£19-50

ORGANISATIONAL INNOVATION

Organisational Innovation

Competitive Strategy and the Management of Change in Four Major Companies

KEN STARKEY
*Department of Industrial Economics,
Accounting and Insurance
The University of Nottingham*
ALAN McKINLAY
*Colquhoun Lecturer in Business History
The University of Glasgow*

Avebury

ECONOMIC AND SOCIAL
RESEARCH COUNCIL
E/*S*/*R*/*C*
Work Organisation Research Centre

© K. Starkey and A. McKinlay, 1988

Published by

Avebury

Gower Publishing Company Limited,
Gower House, Croft Road, Aldershot,
Hants. GU11 3HR, England

Gower Publishing Company,
Old Post Road, Brookfield, Vermont 05036
USA

British Library Cataloguing in Publication Data
Starkey, Ken, 1947-
    Organisational innovation.
    1. Companies, Organisational change.
    Management
    I. Title II. McKinlay, Alan, 1957-
    658.4'06

Library of Congress Cataloging-in-Publication Data
Starkey, Ken, 1948-
    Organisational innovation : Competitive strategy and the
management of change in four major companies / Ken Starkey and Alan
McKinlay.
    p.   cm.
    Bibliography: p.
    Includes index.
    1. Organizational change.   I. McKinlay, Alan, 1957-
    II. Title
HD58.8.S7 1988
658.4'06--dc19

ISBN 0 566 05617 8

Printed and bound in Great Britain by
Athenaeum Press Limited, Newcastle upon Tyne

Contents

1 Introduction: organisational innovation

THE NATURE OF ORGANISATIONAL CHANGE

Radical change in organisations is relatively rare. The evolution of organisations has to be understood as a sequence of relatively slow development in a particular direction, punctuated by infrequent major changes of direction:

> organizational histories manifest two principal types of periods. The most common are those in which a particular configuration or orientation is maintained. These are punctuated by brief intervals of broad and concentrated 'quantum' change which can move organizations to a new configuration. (Miller and Friesen 1984, p.xiii).

Organisations are characterised by 'momentum', the tendency to move in one direction and evolve consistently in accordance with a particular perspective, strategy, ideology, and mission of their own. Organisations develop, therefore, according to a particular alignment or configuration of environmental, organisational and strategic variables. The momentum of the existing configuration tends to carry the organisation forward along a particular 'track' where organisational behaviour conforms to particular predictable repertoires of responses.

Transitions, major changes, involve dramatic transformation of existing repertoires.

1

To reverse the trend of evolution and abandon this orientation in the face of every problem would be exceedingly costly and would result in many discrepancies and imbalances. Major stimuli are required to prompt a reversal. ... The price paid for this is sluggish responsiveness to the need to reverse evolutionary trends, and occasional revolutionary periods with all their turmoil, expense, and confusion. (Miller and Friesen 1984, p.264)

Three elements are important in sustaining momentum in an organisation – its meaning systems, its most powerful sub-units and the key environmental contingencies which have to be taken into account in company strategy. These three elements are the key change factors when major transitions are required. The trigger factor in organisational change is likely to be a change in the organisation's environment. The major change problem is the relationship between organisational processes, what goes on inside the organisation (which, in the final analysis, reflects the way in which it is managed), and responsiveness to the organisation's changing environment.

ORGANISATIONAL PROCESSES

The key issue in the management of change is social processes within organisations. The growing concern with organisational processes reflects a reaction against the emphasis on organisational structure as the key determinant of organisational performance. Following Chandler's (1962) seminal study, analysis of organisational change tended to focus on the the relationship between structure and strategy. In the 1970s structural responses to organisational crisis began to appear less than adequate solutions to the problems posed by enormous environmental turbulence. A 'new consensus' began to form around the notion that process variables were at least as important as structural variables.

Waterman, Peters and Phillips examine this new consensus in an essay entitled 'Structure is not organization' (1980). They situate their analysis in a theoretical lineage stemming from the work of Chester Barnard, the cornerstone of which is a concern with the social forces of organisation, and the critique of rational decision-making, planning and organising which formed the substance of classical management theory. Barnard's contribution was the emphasis he placed on the key role of senior management in harnessing these social forces through their role of shaping and guiding values and, thus, creating, maintaining and modifying organisational cultures. One key organisational process, therefore, is culture.

Equally important to the process perspective is the issue of power. It is the problem of maintaining order that raises issues of power and conflict first examined in their organisational effects by Cyert and March (1963). The social order is based on values developed through power struggles (Hill 1981; Weick 1979). Organisations should be viewed as

    political cultures, in which power relations contribute the
    structure and content of cultural forms and the transmission of

ideologies and values is the process by which those forces are legitimated and sustained, or resisted and changed. (Hartley, Kelly and Nicholson 1983, pp.17-18)

Organisational processes become particularly important in times of change. As the business environment becomes less stable an over-emphasis on structure obscures the problem of change. A key managerial concern in a situation of environmental turbulence is to achieve forms of organising which permit rapidity and flexibility of response. What is required in a time of change is a responsive capability nested in a stable culture. Good managers are 'acutely aware of their people's need for a stable, unifying value system - a foundation for long-term continuity'; they construe their task as 'largely one of preserving internal stability while adroitly guiding the organization's response to fast-paced external change' (Waterman, Peters and Phillips 1981, p.51). Such structural changes as are considered necessary are likely to be only one part of an adequate change strategy. It is an important tenet of the new consensus in organisational analysis that organisational effectiveness stems from the interaction of several factors and that effective organisational change depends on change initiatives taking all of these factors onto the agenda for change. Managerial strategies often founder because of their failure to consider the range of factors change involves.

A growing body of research evidence into change indicates that studies in this area need to be historical, contextual and processual. Pettigrew, in his seminal longitudinal analysis of Imperial Chemical Industries (ICI) (Pettigrew, A.M., 1985), argues persuasively that organisational change has to be seen as an ongoing process of continuity and transformation. Organisational history generates a 'framework of opportunity and constraint' (Pettigrew, A.M., 1985, p.26). Pettigrew emphasises the importance of leadership in the change process. The genesis of change often occurs among a small number of people who become aware of a performance gap which they link to a mismatch between environmental change and organisation structure, strategy and culture. The real problem in implementing change is to gain legitimacy for this new perception of the organisation's performance and context thereby

mobilising concern, energy and enthusiasm often in an additive and evolutionary fashion to ... gain powerful support [that will] eventually result in contextually appropriate action. (Pettigrew, A.M., 1985, p.439)

Change, therefore, is a matter not of forcing through an idea against other interest groups' desires but of modifying an idea to harness organisational support, connecting it to 'rising values and environmental priorities, so its power requirements can be assembled' (Pettigrew, A.M., 1985, p.44). Core beliefs concerning an organisations's purpose need to be changed before organisational structures and systems are brought into line with the changed perspective on the organisation's mission. According to Pettigrew, the process of change in ICI depended upon a major adjustment in the core beliefs of top decision-makers and, thus, in company culture. This was followed by changes in company structure with business strategy changes emerging after the changes in culture, structure and systems had been accepted.

Culture, internal politics, organisational structure and organisational context need to be analysed as barriers to action (forces for inertia) but also as essential elements in the production of action (Pettigrew, 1987). Aspects of a firm's context are mobilised by key actors to legitimate agendas for change. Change is to be construed not as a continuous, incremental process but as a pattern of radical/revolutionary change episodes interspersed with periods of incremental adjustment during which changes are stabilised. A key impetus to change at ICI was the effects of the recession on the world chemical market. Stabilisation of the company's changed position involved rationalisation and retrenchment and also a reorientation in the balance of ICI's product portfolio (from heavy to specialty chemicals) and of the company's geographical spread of interests (a move away from concentration in the U.K. to North America and to the Pacific Basin). The periods of radical change were associated with changes in leadership and in the power balance of the organisation as top decision-makers underwent a process of political learning.

A key problem for senior management at ICI was the need to change critical organisational beliefs and, thus, to bring new, more salient problems onto the change agenda. According to the cultural perspective effective organising depends on the negotiation of meaning:

> Reality is selectively perceived, rearranged cognitively and negotiated interpersonally. (Weick 1979, p.164)

The social order of the organisation is constantly being renegotiated; internally (Strauss 1963). According to Weick (1979) organisations are slow to learn, adapt very slowly to change and are dominated by buried assumptions and routine behaviours. Pettigrew argues that organisations are characterised by inertia, an important facet of which is the chronic attachment to false assumptions.

THE NEED FOR INNOVATION

The management of change involves technical, political and cultural factors (Tichy 1982). Change can involve adjustments in any or all of these areas. This creates three kinds of change problem: (a) the technical design problem — 'The organization faces a production problem. Social and technical resources must be arranged so that the organization produces some desired output'; (b) the political allocation problem — 'The organization faces a power- and resource-allocation problem. It must be determined how the organization is used and who reaps its benefits'; and (c) the problem of culture and ideologies — 'Organizations are, in part, held together because people hold similar beliefs about certain important elements. The organization faces the the problem of determining what values need to be held by which people' (Tichy 1982, pp.170-171).

'Triggers' for change include:

4

1. Environmental changes such as increased complexity and unpredictability
2. Technological changes that result in the potential for new products or services and new methodologies for producing existing products and services
3. Shifts in agreement among organizational members over the goals of the organization, as happens when splits erupt among members of the dominant coalition regarding the future mission of the organization
4. Shifts in agreement among organizational members over the means of getting the work done in the organization, as happens when different factions support different forms of production or organizational structure. (Tichy 1982, pp.174-175).

Historically, organisations become 'locked in' to particular traditions or 'design hierarchies' concerning their technical, political and cultural resources (Clark and Starkey 1988). A key problem in understanding change is the character of organisational knowledge concerning these elements of organising. For managers a major change issue is the alignment of factors internal to the firm, such as technology and its human resources, with a changing external environment:

> If any significant internal changes in the organization are to be sustained, it will need to relate to its environment in new ways. (Blackler and Shimmin 1984, p.90)

Faced with the need to 'maintain effective alignments between the organization and its environment' (Miles 1982, p.14) management has three major strategic options: new market strategies; the reorganisation of its organisational structures to cope with changes in its markets; and changes in the production process, including technological and work organisation innovation. The most successful strategy is likely to include elements of all of these.

A growing body of research, emanating from and building upon the important work of Abernathy and his Harvard colleagues on the subject of innovation, has examined how the need for change comes onto the managerial agenda and how it disrupts previous managerial thinking. In a seminal Harvard Business Review article Abernathy, Clark and Kantrow (1981) set out the nature of the new challenge facing Western management. The article analyses the changing nature of industrial competition, particularly from Japan. As a result of this new competition managers are faced with two principal changes: there is increasing exposure to international competition; and technology becomes an increasingly important competitive weapon. The former indicates a need to radically alter traditional Western approaches to production management. The latter requires a new emphasis on technological innovation.

It is the need to change traditional approaches to organising that is more germane to our concerns. We will be concerned with innovations in work organisation rather than in technology. Japan's competitive advantage arises from innovations in work organisation that have given rise to radical improvements in worker productivity and the reliability and quality of products. It does not lie in technological innovation. It is in the area of work organisation that Japan has laid down 'a challenge that ... once seemed beyond the limits of imagination' (Cusumano 1985, p.384). But having said this, we should remember that Japanese competitive advantage does not apply to all industries. In process industries, for example, the subject of one of our later chapters, the Japanese do not possess any competitive edge (Abegglen and Stalk 1986). In other areas of manufacturing, though, the superiority of the Japanese in productivity and quality gives them a major competitive edge which rests, ultimately, on the painstaking attention they pay to design and work organisation (Beynon 1987).

Abernathy, Clark and Kantrow analyse Japan's radically new production management strategies, attributing their competitive advantage to superior 'process yield' – 'an amalgam of management practices and systems connected with production planning and control ... [the] interaction of materials control systems, maintenance practices and employee involvement'. Differences in wage levels add to this but are not the key factor. The key is advantages in production costs and product quality gained by the 'execution of a well-designed strategy based on the shrewd use of manufacturing excellence' and the 'painstaking strategic management of people, materials and equipment, that is, in superior manufacturing performance' (Abernathy, Clark and Kantrow 1981, p. 74).

In a later work, Industrial Renaissance. Producing a competitive future for America (1983), Abernathy and colleagues elaborate on this argument:

> Japanese producers use less capital to produce a vehicle than do their U.S. competitors and can sustain a given volume of production with much lower levels of investment. ... The Japanese advantage rests not on substitution of capital for labor or labor for capital; it rests, instead, on diligent control of the whole system of production. (p.62)

> Japanese manufacturing systems keep their lines operational a higher percentage of the time, make greater use of materials-handling equipment, process fewer defective parts, enjoy lower rates of worker absenteeism, and match workers better with their tasks. These strengths ... are all the direct result of a production philosophy that stresses not volume ... but quality – of process as well as product. (p.79)

The authors also highlight the lessons for Western management. Western manufacturers, they argue, have 'lost touch with the notion that skill in production, not just in marketing and finance, could offer a real competitive advantage' (Abernathy, Clark and Kantrow 1983, p.7). They emphasise the importance of excellence in manufacturing and the need to rethink our approach to production management:

> We need to fashion a cogent way of thinking about the complex relations among technology, production management, markets and competition as they change both over historical time and through the course of an industry's evolution. (p.13)

Innovation is of crucial importance here. Innovation

makes obsolete existing capital equipment, labor skills, materials, components, management expertise, and organizational capabilities. It destroys the value of present competence. (p.29)

Innovation is particularly important in the management of social processes and human resources — what Abernathy and colleagues describe as the 'micro software' of corporate management and organisational skills, skills in administration and production management.

Managers must recognize that they have entered a period of competition that requires of them ... a mastery of efficient production, and an unprecedented capacity for work force management. (Abernathy, Clark and Kantrow 1981, p.79)

Management endeavour, therefore, focusses on efficiency and innovation. The tension implicit in this dual focus is encapsulated in the notion of an 'innovation-efficiency dilemma' (Clark and Starkey 1988). Managers have to balance the need for maintaining those elements of current organisation that guarantee efficiency and productivity while innovating in new forms of organisation that will facilitate a long-term competitive strategy.

Abernathy and colleagues point to the need for a radical rethinking of Western thinking about management. This need is corroborated by Halberstam (1987) in his comparison of the evolution of two major automobile manufacturers, Nissan of Japan and Ford of the United States. His story is of the relative decline of the Ford, something Halberstam attributes to a failure in managerial imagination which led to organisational stasis exemplified in the lack of product innovation at Ford. Halberstam lays the blame for this decline on the politics of the company and the relative power positions of different functional groups at Ford:

power moved steadily from the product men, who took risks but were normally the creators of market share, to finance, whose agents knew how to maximise the profits of an existing share in a static industry. (Halberstam 1987, pp.244-245)

With the advent of Japanese competition and the oil shock of the early 1970s the automobile industry became anything but 'static' and Ford found itself faced with growing problems.

INNOVATION IN WORK ORGANISATION

During the last decade there have been strong pressures for change in British industry. Recession, increased competition, market uncertainty, an accelerating trend in new technological developments (new manufacturing plant and information technology) and, now, an upturn of trade in the 1980s have all contributed to management's need to critically evaluate previously accepted modes of organising work. A changing labour market situation, with high unemployment and an

7

alteration in the industrial relations climate has provided an opportunity to introduce change in the employee relations sphere. Combined with the turbulence and uncertainty in market domains, changes in the labour market have created a 'strategic window' for adaptive action (Miles 1982). The growing inadequacy of conventional wisdom in generating solutions to the major problems facing organisations has necessitated changes in managerial practices.

For many firms the recession of the 1970s saw a mixture of reduced demand, increased competition and decreased market share against a background of volatile commodity markets (particularly oil) and poor industrial relations (Child 1977). The effects of international competition, especially from the Far East 'where efficiency, quality and flexibility demonstrably exceeded anything which had been achieved in Britain' (British Institute of Management 1985, p.7), were exacerbated by the 'British disease' — low productivity, poor product quality, inadequate control of labour costs and weak management (Marsden, Morris, Willman and Wood 1985, p.175). British management found itself faced with increasing competitive pressures in a fast-changing market-place and a growing realisation that its traditional approach to motivating employees was no longer successful. It also found itself hampered by inherited ways of thinking about managing and particular organisational forms in which the tendency to bureaucracy led to slow and inflexible decision-making which exacerbated the problem of becoming more sensitive to a fast-changing competitive environment.

The general context of innovations in work organisation, the subject of this study, then, is markets characterised by over-capacity and declining demand (Confederation of British Industry 1985) and a motivation problem — how to motivate employees to behave in ways that are competitive. Against this background management has to develop market strategies to ensure competitiveness. These strategies have to be enacted in forms of work organisation which will 'enable' the competitive response (Sir Adrian Cadbury, quoted Tse 1985, p.131). Key issues include the ability to produce and market attractive products, the nature of the skills base necessary to sustain change in an increasingly difficult to predict market-place, technological change, and the forms of management necessary to create and sustain competitive advantage in these areas.

The Organization of Work Panel of the British Institute of Management (BIM), in a study of innovation in work organisation, highlights the need for such innovations to reflect changing market circumstances (BIM 1985). There is an important link between business strategy and work organisation. The management role in work organisation 'involves many aspects in the process of adapting an organization to its markets' (BIM 1985, p.1). A recent NEDO report (NEDO 1986, p.6) also links business strategy and manning practices.

Three common themes linking business strategy to manning practices were observed: a perceived need to improve the responsiveness of all factors of production to changes in business requirements; a shift towards decentralisation as a means of doing so; and a reluctance to increase the number of employees in the process.

The current priority of managerial strategy has been conceptualised as the search for organisational flexibility. Declining overall demand and the increasing volatility and diversity of consumer demand has called established marketing and production strategies into question. Until the mid-seventies managerial strategy was predicated on maximising economies of scale through a highly integrated division of labour and the maintenance of control through 'scientific management', the use of specialised machinery 'dedicated' to the mass production of standard products and elaborate hierarchical management structures. Scientific management was based on the use of scientific methods to study work and to determine the simplest principles of job design. It required the shifting of all responsibility for thinking about work organisation to management away from workers. Above all the intention was that 'managers should do all the thinking relating to the planning and design of work, leaving the workers with the task of implementation' (Morgan 1986, p.30). Implementation was based on conformity with management rules and performance tightly controlled by managerial monitoring. Increasingly, however, production systems based on dedicated capital equipment and tightly specified jobs have proved incapable of responding to the challenges thrown up by a fast changing marketplace. The Japanese competitive edge, for example, was generated by efficiency, quality and flexibility previously unachievable in Britain.

It has been suggested that the 1980s constitute a transition period in organisational behaviour that will mean the end of Fordism and scientific management as dominant paradigms of work organisation. Fordism, the approach to work organisation pioneered by Henry Ford, describes the mechanisation of production, the use of specialised machinery and the mass production of a standardised product by closely supervised, semi-skilled labour for sale in mass consumer markets. It combines the fragmentation of work, close supervision of machine-paced work, emphasis on the right to manage and the payment of high day rates (Marsden, Willman and Wood 1985, pp. 180-181). It is inherently inflexible. Moves towards flexibility in work organisation have been conceptualised in terms of a trend towards 'flexible specialisation'. 'Flexible specialisation' refers to an integrated marketing, investment and production strategy which lies at the interface of product standardisation and customisation. Through the judicious mix of flexible computerised production and the sub-contracting of standardised component manufacture companies hope to balance economies of scale and economies of scope in novel organisational configurations (Sabel 1982).

Flexible specialisation, it is argued, has come onto the managerial agenda because declining overall demand and increasing volatility and diversity of demand have called established marketing and production strategies, predicated on Fordist systems of management, into question, thus creating new constraints on managerial goals (Sabel 1982). Business strategy must now attempt to reconcile production and marketing strategies by balancing economies of scale against economies of scope. The extent of experimentation with new forms of flexible manufacture is correlated to the rapidity of decline and diversification in the marketplace. The overriding managerial problem according to the flexible specialisation scenario is the reduction of the cost of producing an extended and, in relative terms, a fast-changing product range. This replaces the previous managerial imperative of Fordism — the minimisation of the average cost of the production of a narrow product range by an extended division of labour, scientific management and tight control of the labour process. The key organisational task, therefore, focusses on a portfolio of associated rather than standardised products, limited batch sizes and short to medium product runs. The need is for versatile workers with all-round skills. This demands high-trust relations between managers and workers and the constant updating of skills.

The need for increased flexibility and responsiveness to changing market needs affects work organisation in two ways. Either, production of core products is rationalised and intensified and fewer workers are used more productively. And/or, product diversification entails reskilling through the breakdown of demarcation lines and job enlargement. The precise mix of these processes is dependent upon a host of contingent factors. Capital investment tends to complement the reskilling process where new technologies such as CAD/CAM (Computer Aided Design/Computer Aided Manufacture) tend to erode divisions between craftsman and technician and between design and production. In the labour process the key emphasis is on rationalisation — a move towards a 'lean organisation', the search for efficiency through new working practices, the intensification of work and the reduction of labour costs. For core labour forces the dominant trend in job redesign is towards flexible specialisation with a new emphasis on training. In the introduction of new technology the key managerial concern is the choice between economies accruing to capital investment, the flexibility new technology can provide and the economies achievable through the more flexible use of labour as an alternative to major capital investment in a period of market uncertainty. To increase labour productivity more flexible ways of organising time have also been introduced — the reorganisation of rotas and shift systems, flexi-time, part-time and temporary working. New ways of contracting time are accompanied by new ways of contracting out for labour as an alternative to expanding the firm's core labour force. In terms of overall manpower trends the change seems to be towards the rationalisation of existing manning levels (in both employee and managerial groups) towards a 'leaner, fitter' core in which the highest necessary level of skills is encouraged and developed.

According to a NEDO report, firms in four sectors — engineering, food and drink manufacturing, retail distribution and financial services — were introducing changes designed 'to fit more precisely the demand for labour to its supply, improve productivity and the use of capital equipment, reduce overtime and encourage employees to acquire further skills', as a way of adjusting to changing market demands (NEDO 1986, p.iv). Similarly, the Organization of Work Panel of the British Institute of Management, composed of representatives from self-consciously innovative companies, suggests that there is a new pattern of changes in work organisation emerging in leading firms that focusses on attacking rigidities in working methods, in the production process, in existing skill structures, in the organisation of working time and in managerial practices. The Panel argues that work organisation change centres on two main issues:

1. Work reorganisation aiming at the more flexible use of skills – the 'flexing' of the labour process. This also encompasses: rationalisation and reduction in numbers employed, both staff and labour; the introduction of new technology; the more flexible use of time; and more flexible ways of managing the production process such as 'just in time' and 'spinning off', the more flexible use of contracting.

2. Work reorganisation aiming at organisational and managerial 'flexing': the introduction of more flexible approaches to management and organisation, more flexible organisational structures, an alteration of the balance between centralisation and decentralisation, and changes in organisational culture – in short, a reorganisation of the managerial process.

The prime need, the Panel argues, is 'flexibility and the ability to respond quickly to all kinds of pressures' (British Institute of Management 1985, p.25).

Flexibility has several aspects. Operational flexibility describes an organisation's ability to respond effectively and efficiently to changes in production volume as demand waxes and wanes. Strategic flexibility describes the capacity that exists

when the firm is easily able to change the composition of all the product market combinations by renewal of products, by switching to new markets or different technologies, by acquisition of other firms or divestment of nonviable or, on the basis of new perspectives, unwished for parts of existing activities. (Krijnen 1985, p.69)

Structural flexibility describes the ability to affect transitions between appropriate organisational structures as the environment demands, combining existing departments or creating new ones.

The quicker and the more unpredictably the environment changes the greater the need for flexibility (Mascarenhas 1985). Standardisation and its concomitant inflexibility will suffice in an environment of little competition and stable customer demand. But inflexible organisational features such as skill specialisation, clear objectives, unambiguous authority structures, and standard operating procedures with explicit decision criteria are likely to be maladaptive in an environment that is changing. An unstable environment favours flexibility and organic structures, a stable environment rigid mechanistic structures (Burns and Stalker 1961). Flexibility means that there are a variety of alternative control measures available at times of crisis.

Innovations in work organisation aim to increase the cost-effective use of human resources:

the need to change the span and quantity of competences of a company's human resources to match the requirements of the market and new technologies has resulted in a need to rethink how people are employed, organized and developed. ... [This has led to] restructuring with the broad objective of increasing the cost-effective use of human resources, strengthening site and business identity, developing team based commitment to the objectives of the business, eliminating all artificial divisions between employee groups, and generally improving the quality of working life and employee relations. (Cross 1985, p.35)

In employee relations the trend is away from an emphasis on control to one of commitment (Walton 1985; Guest 1986). Developments in the American automobile industry, so long synonymous with conflictual employee relations, exemplify this trend. The recent agreements between the Union of Automobile Workers and Ford Motor Company demonstrate the first stirrings of a sense of mutuality of interests and the need to transcend old antagonisms (Katz, 1985). The nature of the employment contract becomes increasingly important:

work rules and job classifications, typically insurance against job loss and erosion of skilled work, eventually come to be viewed as 'inefficient' and 'cumbersome' when productivity issues emerge under the guise of simplifying work. The predictable traditional collective bargaining agreements negotiated under the more stable economic conditions impedes management's ability to respond to fluctuations in the market. (Giordano 1986, pp.34–35)

Cross compares traditional and new forms of work organisation. The traditional is characterised by maximum task breakdown into narrow skill bands, with external control of work administered by supervisors and specialist staff according to established procedures all arranged according to a tall organisation chart, managed in autocratic style in a climate that does not encourage risk-taking. The new form has tasks grouped in the most appropriate fashion based on multiple broad skills. Control is internal, based on self-regulation (individual and autonomous or quasi-autonomous groups). The organisation chart is flat, management style participative, and innovation is encouraged.

As the business environment becomes more complex, uncertain and varied, the structure of the organisation has to become more complex (Astley and Van de Ven 1983) but structural complexity has to be carefully managed to avoid the rigidities it can create. As a leading British manager expressed it: 'There is no way to avoid some sort of bureaucracy – but you have to loosen the organization' (Sir Adrian Cadbury, quoted Minkes and Nuttall 1984, p.19). New processes become necessary to supplement rules and hierarchy (Galbraith 1973). Decentralisation may be necessary to offset the inflexibility of referring decisions to the centre. Lateral processes can be more effective than vertical in increasing the organisation's information-processing and decision-making capacities (Galbraith 1973). There are moves away from functional rigidity in the transition from function to matrix as a means of speeding up responsiveness by improving coordination between functions (Child 1984, p.103). As product demands change quickly, the market becomes uncertain, the relationship between product and market more difficult to decode, competitors innovate in technology, a new managerial emphasis is needed, a move from a 'logic of control' to a 'logic of change' (Kolodny 1979, p.549). Product innovation, particularly, increases the need for lateral relations between product manager and the rest of the organisation (Galbraith 1973).

The use of lateral relations - direct contact, liaison roles, task forces, and teams - permits the organization to make more decisions and process more information without overloading hierarchical communication channels. These channels are reserved for the unique consequential problems, which increase in number as uncertainty and diversity of the task increase. Further increases in task uncertainty and diversity result in more decision making at lower levels through joint decision processes. (Galbraith 1973, p.89)

It will be remembered that the matrix form of organisation design emerged in the highly innovative aerospace and electronics industries.

Decisions are devolved downwards to autonomous groups, rather than diffused upwards through the hierarchy. The effectiveness, productivity and capacity of bureaucratic forms of organising work are seen as having exhausted themselves and, therefore, as being inadequate for current economic and market contingencies, i.e., environmental conditions of turbulence, uncertainty, and complexity. The trend is towards debureaucratisation and dehierarchisation, the building in of innovation, flexibility and adaptability 'in the face of external turbulence, threat and overload':

tasks and activities become the new organizing principle of the managerial labour process, as opposed to the rigid role structure of hierarchical authority and spheres of competence. (Heydebrand 1983, p.106)

Rigid divisions of managerial labour are broken down through management development so that managerial skills become more broadly based while rooted in an emphasis on business skills and the need to increase responsiveness to the customer/client, and thus to the market. This suggests a move away from centralised hierarchies - at the very least their slimming down - towards more flexible organisational arrangements. Relationships between the centre and the rest of the organisation change. New divisional structures more responsive to environmental pressures might be established, control increasingly devolved to these new organisational structures. Organisational processes are also made more flexible - more highly participative.

Kanter sums up these developments:

The organizations now emerging as successful will be, above all, flexible; they will need to be able to bring particular resources together quickly, on the basis of short-term recognition of new requirements and the necessary capacities to deal with them. They will be organizations with more 'surface' exposed to the environment and with a whole host of sensing mechanisms for recognizing emerging changes and their implications. ...

Until now, most organizations have attempted to deal with forthcoming change and with environmental contingencies by ever-more elaborate mechanisms for strategic planning — essentially designed to help organizations feel in control of their futures. There will always be a need for this, of course, but the balance between planning — which reduces the need for effective reaction — and structural flexibility — which increases the capacity for effective reaction — needs to shift toward the latter. The era of strategic planning (control) may be over; we are entering an era of tactical planning (response). (Kanter 1985, p.41)

There is a growing emphasis on creating an organisational culture which is flexible enough to generate commitment and speed of response to the changing environment. This trend is best exemplified in the success of Peters and Waterman's In Pursuit of Excellence (1982). According to these authors excellent organisations are characterised by the ability to change. They are 'continuously innovative', geared to 'quick action and regular experimentation':

Innovative companies are especially adroit at continually responding to change of any sort in their environments. ... As the needs of their customers shift, the skills of their competitors improve, the mood of the public perturbates, the forces of international trade realign, and government regulations shift, these companies tack, revamp, adjust, transform, and adapt. In short, as a whole culture, they innovate. (Peters and Waterman 1982, p.12)

They recognise the customer as the key element in the organisation's environment. Top management's key role is to shape organisational culture by managing the values of the organisation.

Hickman and Silva (1984), in an extension of Peters and Waterman's work, argue the need for managers to combine strategy and culture in seeking change by analysing customers and employers:

While strategic thinking aims at getting and keeping customers, culture building attracts, develops, motivates, and unifies the right kind of employees. ... no matter how strongly an organization's culture motivates and develops employees, if customers do not perceive better products and services as a result, the culture has been wasted. The intertwined relationship between customers and employees requires watchful management, by well-trained executives. (Hickman and Silva 1984, pp.85-86)

The main aim of strategy is the decoding and satisfaction of customer needs thus gaining advantage over competitors, Culture has to do with employees and the development of commitment to a common purpose and the competence to deliver superior performance. Excellent organisations build and sustain excellent cultures by 'selecting, motivating, rewarding, retaining and unifying good employees'. 'Soft' people skills are, therefore, as or more important than hard quantitative skills (Hickman and Silva 1984, p.69). The goal is an organisation 'of many hands but of one mind devoted to building the best product possible, fully satisfying customers and taking care of one's own people' (Hickman and Silva 1984, pp.64-65). A major managerial goal is to instill commitment to the common culture and to reward competence. Motivation is important. People want to be 'stretched'. Employees 'relish' challenges to their competence.

To implement a successful culture and successful change it is a prerequisite that leaders are respected. There are two essential preconditions for change:

   a felt need and a respected other ... before meaningful, lasting change can occur a need for it must be felt throughout the organization. By respected other we mean some individual or group of individuals respected within or outside the organization who must advocate the change. (Hickman and Silva 1984, pp.209-210)

Change has to be defined in terms congruent with an organisation's strategy and culture and in terms of the management structures, management attitudes, employees, employee attitudes, skills and operating systems which need to be changed.

The key role of top managers becomes one of 'changing the cognitive, strategic and power orientation' of their organisations (Prahalad and Doz 1984, pp.373-4). A major problem is to 'meld' human resources planning and management with strategic planning (Szilagyi and Schweiger 1984). Not only are strategic choice of product markets and the creation of corporate structures inseparable:

   there is certainly a level of administrative decision which is as much a strategic preoccupation of top management as is the choice of products and markets. (Minkes and Nuttall 1985, p.6)

These have to be assimilated to managerial strategies concerning work organisation. There is a symbiotic relationship between strategy, markets and work organisation in the dual sense of the organisation of managerial and labour process.

CONCLUSION

The central focus of our study is organisational innovation in four major companies - the Ford Motor Company, Pilkington Brothers, Rank Xerox and Shell U.K. The experiences of these companies demonstrate managers in the process of learning to cope with problems of market change and new competitive conditions by aligning different elements of organisation, striving to learn from and to undo the mistakes of the past, unsure of the future but attempting to create working practices which they anticipate will enable them to cope with its uncertainties. We have emphasised work organisation as a key element of this endeavour. By this we mean the organisation of the work of employees and the management of the production process by management and also the organisation of managerial work itself.

Changes in work organisation within our case companies are essentially market-driven, that is, they originate in responses to changing product markets. New business strategies necessitate the rethinking of previous forms of work organisation. Managerial initiatives focus on the analysis of product markets, the organisation of shopfloor work (manpower levels, skills, time), reward structures, relationships with suppliers, technological innovation, organisational structure, managerial style and organisational culture. Strategy implementation emerges as an arena for managerial learning. The process of implementation is characterised by negotiation, compromise and, on occasion, conflict of views between management and employees.

While our major concern will be work organisation we wish to emphasise that work organisation is only one of the factors that need to be analysed if organisational change is to be adequately understood. To concentrate only on working practices tells only part of the story. We attempt to avoid the major problem of much labour process/industrial relations literature – its over-emphasis upon production at the expense of product markets – by emphasising the increasingly symbiotic link between problems of business strategy, corporate survival, efficiency and competitiveness (Beynon 1987). The important conceptual link to be established is that which joins the company's production system, managerial process and market context.

It is, therefore, the interaction of work organisation with other factors that is the key theoretical and practical issue that we wish to analyse. Studies of the automobile industry have demonstrated the potential of this more sophisticated approach to work organisation. Whipp and Clark (1985) demonstrate that the problems of the British car industry stem not just from labour relations problems but from inadequate capital investment, inadequate product development, and poor and badly integrated management practices. Williams, Williams and Haslam (1987) critically evaluate Austin Rover's over-concentration on work organisation and the reform of working practices. They demonstrate that a more fundamental problem facing the company, one its senior managers failed to adequately address, was its market strategy and the need to produce new attractive products. Work organisation, therefore, is not the only problem to be resolved. But work organisation is important. Marsden, Morris, Willman and Wood (1985) demonstrate that changes in employee relations have major effects on the competitiveness of car firms and, thus, do contribute to the search for competitive advantage.

The data on which our study is based is extracted from the final project of the ESRC Work Organization Research Centre's (WORC) programme. The WORC programme adopted a longitudinal, comparative focus based on eight in-depth studies of firms in their sectoral environments. In this project we selected firms whose representatives constituted the Organization of Work Panel of the British Institute of Management (British Institute of Management 1985). These firms constitute a self-selected group of companies self-consciously experimenting with new patterns of work organisation. Visits were made to each of these firms where personnel directors or senior personnel managers reporting directly to the board participated in semi-structured interviews. The interview schedule (see Appendix) focussed on the stimuli that gave rise to the need for changes in work organisation and the dynamics and politics of the change process. In particular, we investigated the internal and external sources of the change strategy and its relation to shifts in marketing strategy. The schedule was administered by the the WORC research team to approximately forty senior managers. All quotations in the text, unless otherwise attributed, are drawn from these interviews which were, in the majority of cases, tape-recorded. The interview data was supplemented by site visits to familiarise the authors with the nature of the firms' production processes and by data collected from company reports, internal company documents, the business press and other academic studies.

2 Ford Motor Company

INTRODUCTION

Since the launch of the Model T automobile in 1908, the Ford Motor Company has become synonymous with a particular way of doing business - Fordism. Fordism is a short-hand term for the pattern of organising Ford pioneered, based on simplified production methods, standardised products and a highly centralised management structure. In essence, Henry Ford's company established a template for mass production and mass marketing which remained virtually intact for over fifty years. The durability of the Ford organisational template rested on the comparative stability of the world's auto markets and the absence of revolutionary innovations either in car technology or productive techniques. Until the mid-seventies, predictable patterns of demand and competition and slow change in production methods allowed Ford and the other major auto companies to maintain organisational stability. Organisational fine tuning rather than radical restructuring was the key to sustaining profitability.

The question addressed by this chapter is, how has the company, specifically its British subsidiary, responded to the challenge of a changing market place and new competitors, particularly the Japanese. For auto manufacturers, the last decade has irreversibly upset the established verities upon which success had been based. Direct competition across the full range of car sizes has fragmented a near-saturated market and forced Ford to refine their traditional perception of the market place as relatively homogeneous and consumers' primary choice criterion as cost. Not only is consumer choice more varied but it is also increasingly volatile and difficult to predict beyond the short-term. In this fast-moving environment organisational responsiveness is at a premium. At the same time, technological innovations have compressed the time lag between design and production and reduced the point at which manufacturers derive full economies of scale. Both processes, market shifts and technical change, have made organisational flexibility central to competitive advantage. The task for Ford senior management has been to reorganise the company's human resources to maximise organisational responsiveness in the short-term and to firmly embed change as a permanent feature of working – and managing – for Ford.

THE CAR INDUSTRY: A PERIOD OF TRANSITION

The central principles of Fordism remained intact until the early 1970s. Indeed, in the decades since Ford introduced mass auto production the basic model of standardised products and simplified production was diffused, in modified fashion, throughout the world auto industry. In the early 1970s the slowdown of the Western economies and the growing saturation of the principal car markets stimulated increased competition for export markets. The major auto companies no longer abstained from the core markets of their international rivals (Tolliday and Zeitlin 1986, pp.11–13). Against this backdrop the oil shocks of 1974 and 1979 reversed the upward spiral of world demand which had prevailed since the war. More than this, the oil crises altered the composition of demand towards smaller, more fuel efficient cars. Over-capacity, faltering growth and increasingly differentiated demand not only intensified competition but also altered the terms of inter-company rivalry. From 1979, worldwide demand converged around small, fuel efficient models, a fact which integrated the world market to an unprecedented extent. 'Suddenly', as Altshuler, Anderson, Jones, Roos and Womack (1984, p.7) put it, 'every manufacturer was a potential threat to every other manufacturer'. To this already turbulent environment was added one further destabilising ingredient: the Japanese challenge.

For almost thirty years after 1945 Japanese car producers, their domestic market sheltered by government protectionism, perfected production systems based on minimising the threshold at which scale economies were achieved at each stage of manufacture. Each of the organisational innovations which now give Japanese auto companies their competitive edge were developed in response to particular problems rather than part of a grand strategy. Thus, the life-time employment enjoyed by the core employees of major companies was the response to post-war unionisation and labour unrest. Over the following three decades relationships between employers, managers and workers were transformed from the adversarial to co-operative, based on mutual identification with company goals and communal effort. 'Just in Time' (JIT) production, which cuts down buffer stocks at each stage of the assembly process, was developed to combat the chronic low quality of Japanese production. A neglected feature of JIT is that it compels managers to continually introduce minor innovations in manufacturing processes. This inherent principle of JIT management is given further momentum by the truncated life cycles of Japanese products and medium batch production. Unlike the vertically integrated organisations developed by the major Western auto companies, Japanese assemblers stimulated networks of specialist suppliers to lessen their dependence on imported components. By the early 1970s the combined effect of these innovations had placed the Japanese auto industry at the forefront of manufacturing techniques. It was to take the seismic changes in the structure of the world auto market of the 1970s to reveal the enormous strength Japanese manufacturers derived from these profound organisational innovations.

Western car manufacturers initial interpretations of the new competitive conditions of the late 1970s reaffirmed the validity of the Fordist model of production and company organisation. In the second half of the 1970s all the transnational Western companies pursued variants of the 'world car' strategy which would seek to maximise scale economies by producing and marketing standardised small cars on a global scale. Tolliday and Zeitlin (1986, p.16) explain the logic of this strategy:

> the American producers in particular based their strategy on the diagnosis ...that international demand for cars was converging around a narrow range of models. They believed that the rise in oil prices necessitated a once and for all design shift towards smaller cars which would be even more standardized than their predecessors. This shift would revive the possibility of further economies of scale and cost reductions through the introduction of new forms of dedicated automation and the relocation of labour-intensive phases of production in low-wage areas abroad.

The 'world car' strategy was classical Fordism writ large: not merely on a national or multi-national scale but globally. All the major companies have been forced to pull back from the full implications of this ambitious strategy. While there has been a worldwide shift towards smaller vehicles this has been accompanied by increased demand for product differentiation. Moreover, the 'world car' strategy exacerbated the internal problems associated with Fordism. The scale of global production and marketing magnified Fordism's immense problems of coordination and communication: rigid hierarchies and slow decision-making processes combined to produce organisational atrophy during a period in which organisational responsiveness was fast becoming the critical factor deciding competitive advantage.

For Abernathy (1978), the world auto industry is currently in a transitional period as momentous as the founding of the modern industry in the first decades of the twentieth century. The long period of stability in which the major auto companies consolidated their dominant positions was characterised by slow growth of demand for a well-defined and technologically stable product. Manufacturing technologies displayed a similar stability, evolving incrementally with no radical innovations to upset the competitive equilibrium. During the current transitional phase the world auto industry is, argues Abernathy (1978), poised between 'maturity' and 'dematurity': between stable and volatile trading environments; between organisational and technological stasis and a novel environmental pressure for organisational responsiveness. The current transition has been impelled by the decomposition of mass markets, the emergence of the organisational challenge issued by Japanese companies and by technical change, specifically the creation of new automated manufacturing systems based on adaptable rather than dedicated machinery.

Ford regard the 1980s as a watershed period in its history, a time when the company has started to question its traditional approach to marketing, production and human resource management. Above all, Ford are becoming conscious that sustained profitability in a ferociously competitive market environment requires significant productivity and quality improvements within a context of increased organisational flexibility. Achieving these strategic priorities is dependent upon the success of wholesale work reorganisation and a move towards co-operative rather than adversarial labour relations. In short, profound organisational change is at the core of Ford's competitive strategy.

> Change is a permanent feature of the motor industry, but its present phase must rank as the most fluid since the earliest years. The process of restructuring within and between companies is bound to continue: our objective must be to manage and control our part of that process. (Ford Motor Company Annual Report, 1985)

The shift in Ford's competitive strategy has impacted upon the company's design philosophy. Ford's traditional marketing and production strategies placed a high premium on design continuity. For Lorenz (1986), Ford has undergone 'a conversion of Galileo-like proportions', through which consumer tastes for the first time superceded the interests of the production engineer. Product design and the the ability to think not in terms of 'an amorphous mass market' but in terms of distinct market segments with products targetted specifically at these segments became a key competitive weapon (Lorenz 1986, p.3). New computer systems enable the speedier communication of information about market performance between dealers and Ford have accelerated responsiveness to market changes.

Robert Lutz, former Ford of Europe President, explained the reasons for this strategic reorientation:

> [The strategy is] to get Ford cars out there that people desperately want, rather than cars they will buy because they are the lowest priced on the market. You can't do that any more because the Japanese have taken that part of the market away from us. [They] have taken over the no-nonsense, no-frills, high-value for money, reliable transportation part of the market. My goal is to be a mass producer of the type of cars BMW and Mercedes have a reputation for making. We are moving up in technology and credibility so we get the same price elasticity as they have., (quoted Lorenz 1986, p.91)

The result of this strategic choice has been the incorporation of innovative car technologies in model derivatives 'extending the Ford product range into areas of refinement previously not available in the mass market' (Annual Report, 1985). Implementing this new design philosophy involved integrating product development across previously inviolate functional boundaries. In turn, this organisational innovation challenged the functional hierarchies whose inherent inertial qualities were exacerbated by the dominance of the finance function with its emphasis on short-term returns. As we shall see, it remains to be seen if Ford can maintain the momentum of organisational change begun in the early 1980s.

THE NEED FOR CHANGE

Ford Motor Company Limited - Ford Britain - is a vehicle manufacturing company and a wholly owned subsidiary of Ford Motor Company of Detroit. The U.S. parent exercises certain financial controls such as the approval of spending over certain limits but, in essence, the management of their day-to-day operations is left to the Ford subsidiaries.

> Pay bargaining responds to local conditions and, although we need the formal approval of Detroit, our judgement on what fits local conditions is generally backed. Our recent two-year pay deal, for example, was made without any pressure from America in favour of such long-term contracts. (Roots 1986, p.1)

The automotive activities of Ford Motor Company Ltd. are coordinated with those of the other European Ford subsidiaries by Ford of Europe, 'to maximise economies of scale and minimise duplication of effort in the European market' (British Institute of Management 1985, p.7).

The 1970s saw major changes in the company's market situation to which, as one senior manager put it, Ford, in its 'rich complacency,' did not pay sufficient attention. An emerging problem was growing Japanese competition and the standards of efficiency and quality of product the Japanese were able to achieve. In the European and the U.S. car markets this led to increasing Japanese market penetration, increased market saturation and a harder fight for market share. In the U.K. Ford continued to dominate the market, regularly leading new car sales figures and dominating the fleet and commercial vehicles business, but market domination was not always reflected in its profit margins. Fierce competition depressed prices. Demand became increasingly sensitive to price and marketing costs came to be seen as excessive.

Problems in the market-place were exacerbated by internal problems. British plants were characterised by poor productivity and efficiency, poor labour relations and a consistent failure to meet production schedules. The Japanese threat, therefore, emerged as the new factor compounding the internal problems of the company. A key management goal became the reduction of the company's breakeven through reducing fixed costs which meant, essentially, reducing labour costs through rationalisation and improving efficiency.

The 1980s are seen as a watershed by the company, a time when the it started to question its traditional approach to management, responding to: increasing competitive pressures from elsewhere in Europe, and more especially from the Japanese automotive industry where efficiency, quality and flexibility demonstrably exceeded anything which had been achieved in Britain; the changing economic and social environment; and a growing realisation that the traditional approach was no longer the most effective way of getting the best out of the company's employees. This realisation has led to a wide range of work reorganisation initiatives aimed at improving productivity and two major change programmes – 'After Japan' and a programme of Employee Involvement/Participative Management.

1985 is seen as a turning point in company's recent history as the effects of these change initiatives began to make themselves felt. The years 1981 to 1984 had seen a steady decline in profits, with 1984 seeing an actual operating loss after tax. The Sierra, Ford's major model in the medium-sized, family saloon and fleet sector, launched in 1982, met with a mixed response and needed major financial support. In 1984 Ford was faced with 'heavy discounting [to retain market share], soaring marketing costs and a shortfall in the funds necessary for future manufacturing and product investment' (Annual Report, 1984). Excess capacity reduced returns on investment.

1985 marked a 'substantial turnaround' with a return to profitable operation. This turnaround was founded on a strategy of pursuing a 'high, profitable volume of business' rather than a strategy of 'maximum sales at any cost' (Annual Report, 1985). Manufacturing performance improved, many fewer vehicles were lost through industrial disputes, and an increase in output, measured in terms of vehicles produced per employee, was welcomed as reflecting an improvement in productivity, indicating a measure of success in the company's long-term plans for greater efficiency. In 1986 productivity gains were sustained in Ford's British plants as were cost reductions and efficiency improvements. Production schedules improved markedly. Sales increased though profits suffered as a result of adverse currency fluctuations. In 1987 it was announced in the press that the company planned to expand car production in the U.K. with the creation of possibly 1000 new jobs and moves to recommence the export of British-made cars to the continent. In fact, the company states that this is a possibility rather than a firm plan. The fact, though, that it is even being considered reflects the company's positive response to the changes it has been able to make in the area of work organisation – reflected in the fact that it is now building to schedule in the U.K. for the first time for 10 years.

INNOVATIONS IN WORK ORGANISATION

One of the major barriers to change at Ford has been the legacy of the company's chequered industrial relations history. Ford management's traditional low trust approach to labour relations was superimposed on the inherent conservatism of the British car industry whose combination of competitive multi-unionism and sectional shopfloor bargaining tends to dissipate radical initiatives. The company's resultant industrial relations problems have been analysed elsewhere (Beynon 1984). What is important to the concerns of our study is the emergence, from the mid-1970s onwards, of a growing recognition that winning employee endorsement of collective agreements was essential to the long-term stabilisation of labour relations and the enhancement of productivity. However, continuing industrial unrest at plant-level seriously hampered production continuity and threatened to become a critical competitive handicap. The task for Ford senior management was to devise structures and processes which would involve shopfloor representatives in some responsibility for production and efficiency.

A key gain in the 1980s, according to senior Ford management, has been a change in the British workforce's attitude towards work and conflict at work based on a growing acceptance of the harsh economic reality the company faces. This change of attitude marks a potential sea change in the history of Ford industrial relations, traditionally marked by conflict, mistrust and basic opposition between labour and management. The company entered the 1980s with a growing sense that its traditional modes of managing were no longer adequate. A loss of faith in the traditional Ford way of managing (authoritarian, aggressive, confrontational, 'macho') led to a goal of altering the old management style in order

to be less provocative, less brutal and directive.

There was a need felt for a more conciliatory approach, based on the expectation that

there were more effective ways of getting the best out of people than telling them what to do and then having them get on with it. [For example] there were lots of people out there who knew a lot more about putting radiators in cars than anybody else does. We ought to be finding ways and means of drawing on that expertise.

The 1980s has witnessed a major shift in the company's industrial relations strategy in an attempt to accommodate to the presence of trade unions by co-opting them into the managerial process, rather than prolonging what had previously been an essentially antagonistic relationship (Beynon 1984). To this end a whole new process of negotiating was developed, involving not just full-time union officials but shopfloor representatives able to speak for the actual workforce, thus incorporating the company-worker relationship within the formal bargaining procedures and facilitating the communication of agreements and their adherence at the shopfloor level because the workers who would make them work were actually involved in the bargaining process.

Two major change strategies distinguish the 1980s as an important transition period for the company. The first, 'After Japan', was the direct response to the growing awareness of the Japanese competitive lead. Its limited success in Britain is attributed by senior management to union resistance. The second, and continuing, major change initiative centres around Employee Involvement, a labour relations strategy imported from the U.S., and Participative Management, an attempt to change managerial attitudes and traditional ways of managing the company. 'After Japan' began as a response to the lead Japan held in terms of productivity, quality, reliability after a visit to Japan by the head of Ford Europe from which, it has been reported, he returned in a state of shock (Beynon 1987). 'After Japan' involved a major initiative to publicise the company's need to face up

to competition, based on comparison between the productivity levels of
British plants and the productivity and efficiency levels of
competitors. The comparisons were both internal and external.
Externally, the key comparison was with Japan. Internally,
performance in U.K. Ford plants was compared with Ford continental
plants where the same cars are produced on virtually identical
facilities. Thus Halewood and Dagenham were compared, detrimentally,
with Genk and Saarlouis, Ford's plants in Belgium and West Germany,
as a means of motivating the workforce to increase their productivity.

The 'After Japan' 'package' was, essentially, 'a mixture of
financial targets and process changes'(Willman 1986, p.210). The
targets were a minimum return on sales of 5 per cent, a minimum return
on assets of 10 per cent, break-even points for plants of 60 per cent
of capacity and a minimum European market share of 14 per cent. High
standards in work performance were also set and these 'strategic
volume/quality targets related to elements of work reorganization'
(Willman 1986, p.210). A key element of the 'After Japan' campaign
was the attempt to increase employee involvement using quality
circles. Japanese managerial style was interpreted as being based on
taking account of what employees were thinking then seeking consensus
through cooperative managerial strategies that mobilised worker
knowledge and consent. Top-down communication was, thus, matched by
upward communication, maximising inputs of information and learning at
all levels of the organisation.

Quality circles were to function as 'problem-solving workgroups' and
involved training the workforce in problem-solving, skills in
interpersonal relations and self-analysis. One goal here was the
search for consensus in decision-making but this was only 'one plank'
of a 'total' Japanese package embracing Just in Time, the reduction of
inventories, different ways of doing business with suppliers,
statistical process control, operator self-certification, and operator
'seek and repair' to build in quality during the production process
rather than inspect in quality by rectification of defects later.
Central to this endeavour was the communication of market information
to the workforce so as to gradually erode the traditional labour
resistance to managerial messages so that

anything management tells you is by definition untrue.

Approaches similar to quality circles had been demonstrated to work in
the States in initiatives such as QWL (Quality of Working Life) at
General Motors. Quality circles were introduced in Ford in the U.S.
and

as it worked in the States we thought it would be good for us as
well, as is the nature of things in Ford's.

Ford of Europe introduced quality circles in 1979 in order,
primarily, to increase employees' identification with the firm and to
harness their commitment to company objectives. Key process goals
were: to improve the technical efficiency of manufacture thereby
increasing productivity; to stimulate motivation and involvement on
the shopfloor; and to provide a forum for communication between

management and labour thus providing the shopfloor 'with a way of confronting the management's excuses through direct communication' (Financial Times, 26 January 1981). Quality circles were thus seen as a means of developing a motivated and informed workforce; better quality and reliability of product; and cost savings. In terms of Ford managerial culture quality circles represent a transition from a view of motivation as only being amenable to external factors such as pay or control to the creation of intrinsic forms of motivation by involving workers more deeply in the design of work.

So quality circles represent a departure from traditional Western attitudes and organisational patterns in three key respects: they require individuals to operate together as a self-improvement team; they require most managements to adopt a new approach to employee communications and motivation; and they require management, workers and unions to permit the resurgence of the foreman in [a] new role of persuader not policeman. (Lorenz 1981a)

The training necessary to implement the circles provides the workforce with enhanced knowledge about how to resolve production problems through teamwork and knowledge about the company's market situation.

In the U.K., the attempt to introduce quality circles foundered on union resistance. The unions refused to cooperate in the initiative and it was discontinued. There were three main union objections. The company had introduced then without prior discussion. Quality circles were seen as cutting across existing structures for negotiating grievances and they were not just limited to quality problems. The Trade Union Congress (TUC) also opposed quality circles on the grounds that they would undermine existing negotiating structures by by-passing formal channels of communication. The company learned from this experience and is now going about the introduction of employee involvement in a much more gradual way which marks a radical change of managerial style.

Other lessons from Japan were implemented. An important departure was a new approach to quality, exemplified in the change from 'quality control' to 'quality assurance'. Making quality manufacture a key focus of competitive strategy recognised that the Japanese competitive edge rested on the efficient and reliable manufacture of high quality standard products. Ironically Japanese industry had learned its quality lessons from two U.S. experts, Juran and Deming. What it had learnt had enabled it to compete with Western manufacturers on price terms but also in terms of non-price factors such as design, reliability and service. These non-price factors constitute quality (Financial Times, 4 January 1981). Juran attributed the great proportion of product defects, up to 80 per cent, to shortcomings in management. He argued that a top-down training program was necessary to improve quality and that quality should be defined in terms of 'fitness for use', i.e. in terms of the user's appreciation of what constitutes quality. Deming argued that there should be a fundamental change in the approach to quality away from inspection, which led to high rectification costs, towards the prevention of mistakes and the search for methods of product design and manufacture which would promote zero defects.

The new Ford approach to quality is made up of three related sets of ideas. These 'can be separated for the purpose of explanation but they are mutually dependent on one another. In practice, therefore, they are like the three legs of a stool — they can't be introduced separately' (Pettigrew, T.J., 1985, p.81). The three elements are: the process intent approach; Deming's statistical inference methods; and employee involvement. The traditional approach to quality was judged to have failed in the light of Japanese standards because it had been based on detection and correction rather than prevention. Quality had been defined in terms of customer-reported defects and conformity to specification. A new Customer Model of quality replaced this. The new definition of quality was:

> A measurable description of every aspect of a vehicle that a customer can perceive through both inspection and operation, together with the value in each case, which represents his 'threshold of complaint. (Pettigrew, T.J., 1985, p.82)

The process intent approach concentrates on translating customer expectations into measurements that are then translated into improved production process procedures — using the principle that 'what you can't measure, you can't control'. The objective of the the process intent approach is to achieve zero defects:

> This leads to four essential needs at the operation level.
>> Emphasize the outcome rather than the method used to get it: and communicate to the operator what it is and why it matters.
>> Describe the desired outcome using variables which the operator (or the machine in the case of an automatic process) can measure whilst he is doing the work. This way he can guide himself predictably 'home' to an OK outcome every time.
>> This allows the operator to accept the responsibility to assure that the outcome of his operations is OK or — if not — to flag the defect for repair.
>> Periodically measure outcomes and record [them on statistical charts]. Preferably by the operator. Use these to communicate between operators as a tool to improve outcomes and make each other's job easier. (Pettigrew 1985, T.J., p.83)

The Deming statistical inference approach supports the process changes by identifying and reducing random variations in operation outcomes. Deming argues that up to 80 per cent of these random variations are the rectifiable fault of management's failure to analyse and organise the production process in an optimal and achievable fashion. The new approach to quality facilitates design, reduces production and overhead cost, minimises waste, and provides more trouble-free products, thus providing the basis for cost efficiency and better quality of product.

The bulk of training in the new approach is concentrated at the salaried, engineering and foreman level. Among hourly workers it is currently most relevant on the power-train and areas where technological advance has been most pronounced. However, as the technology of final assembly evolves it is likely to become important in this area as well. The long-term tendency in job design, therefore, is towards an enhanced role for shopfloor workers. There are two reasons for this. By virtue of his experience of manufacturing operations the operative has the greatest knowledge about the production process and, secondly, and perhaps most important, 'he and only he can prevent defects' (Pettigrew, T.J., 1985, p.84). It is essential, therefore, to gain the involvement of the production operator in the process of quality assurance. This requires the establishment of high trust relationships between operators and managers. It also requires the dissemination of a common language concerning quality 'to tie everybody's efforts together. Without this language, involvement is difficult, if not impossible' (Pettigrew, T.J., 1985, p.85). This provides the organisation with a 'uniform factual language about outcomes which everybody speaks' (Pettigrew, T.J., 1985, p.87).

The importance the company attaches to the generation of this common language reflects the emphasis it has placed on the task of convincing the workforce of the need for change in working practices. The first step in this task was the communication of information to impress upon the labour force the seriousness of the situation the company was in. The old ways of working were becoming more and more uncompetitive. British productivity was a major problem, British unit labour costs comparing extremely unfavourably not only with the Japanese but also with the company's other factories in Europe. Japanese productivity in the early 1980s was put at five times that of the British. Ford's European plants, a ready source of competitive benchmarking information, were at least twice as productive as their British counterparts. Key elements signalled out in the cost comparisons were downtime in British factories, the consistent failure to meet schedules due to stoppages, and poor product quality and reliability. The major factor contributing to low U.K. productivity compared to its continental counterpart, according to Ford management, has not been the pace of the line, although it is slightly faster on the continent, but interruptions to its continuous flow. The Japanese, as one manager in Ford Europe put it, 'utilise their time so much more efficiently'. A basic difference here was the small number of indirect support workers in Japan, people who inspect finished work, who deliver material to and from the line, minor repairmen. In Japan all these tasks were performed inside the work cycle. At Saarlouis, a factory using similar plant to Halewood to produce the same product, consistency of reaching planned schedules could be relied on, the workforce was flexible and cooperative, stoppages minimal and when repairs were necessary these were effected far faster than in Britain. The ratio of workers directly involved in production to indirects was 1:2 at Saarlouis compared with Halewood's 1:1. Planning was far better on the continent because British management was too preoccupied with industrial relations firefighting. British plants, it was argued, were suffering 'the death of a 1000 cuts'.

As part of the 'After Japan' campaign, the company made a major effort to communicate the productivity facts to the workforce. But perhaps equally effective was a statement made by senior executives that one British plant might be 'an endangered species' unless Ford U.K. changed its way of doing business. A key event in this context was the closure of the foundry at Dagenham, the company's heartland.

This signalled an end to totally integrated production at Dagenham. It also demonstrated the company's seriousness concerning cost-competitiveness. It was considered economic to contract out foundry work rather than invest in new plant to update this facility. The closure constituted 'a cold shower of realisation' and led to a marked change in labour attitudes.

That was the time at which we obtained maximum belief that this was a serious situation. And about that time we started to get the cooperation because a lot of employees suddenly realised that what had happened at the foundry could happen to them too.

The company was able to make previous agreements concerning working practices 'stick' so that efficiency started to improve. Rationalisation measures were carried through. The dialogue now concerned the price of cooperation.

Increasingly the message started to emerge that fellows are willing to cooperate if rewarded.

The change of attitude paved the way for what the company see as a watershed pay agreement of 1985 with its introduction of 'far-reaching' changes in working practices.

The key work organisation elements of the 1985 agreement are: versatility and flexibility, the acquisition of new skills and the elimination of inefficient lines of demarcation. These principles are applied to both craft employees and production operatives. For example, demarcations between electrical and mechanical craftsmen are to be reduced. Flexibility means:

Electrical and mechanical craftsmen must be flexible and versatile across the full range of their respective skills, undertake any electrical or mechanical tasks outside their own trade, subject to capability; undertake tasks such as the preparation of machinery or equipment prior to maintenance work, slinging, the operation of lifting equipment, and driving, where these are feasible. Such craftsmen must also carry out line patrol, taking corrective actions as they identify the need; and be mobile across a plant, or operation. (IDS Report 468, 1986, p.21)

The acquisition of new skills is emphasised. For example, mechanical craftsmen are to be trained in advanced pneumatics and hydraulics. Body and assembly shop employees must be 'fully interchangeable'. Production operators' task may vary with operational needs and they are to be responsible for keeping their work area clean, searching out and repairing defects, and using techniques of quality assurance. Production operators can also be required to assist craft employees in maintenance work. In return for acceptance of the new agreement there was a pay increase of 18.5 per cent for those working on the line with consolidation of attendance bonuses.

Ford had been seeking the kind of changes agreed in the 1985 pay agreement since the beginning of the 1980s. They are implicit in the emulation of Japanese working practices. But the company had been unwilling to pay for them and the unions unwilling to negotiate such changes. The company gradually came to accept the union argument that productivity gains should be linked to pay and also was able to gain acceptance from the unions of principles of work organisation that could not have been achieved even three or four years previously. Wage increase were explicitly linked to efficiency gains. The Company case may be summed up as follows:

> You [the unions] have repeatedly argued across this table that the company needs to buy cooperation with new work practices. Well, we are prepared to discuss that with you now, but we are not interested in forms of words. We have paid for promises before and they have not achieved very much, but if we can find a way of relating pay to more flexible working that really works, we can respond to your claim for more pay. (IDS Report 461, 1985, p.4)

The 1985 agreement provided for the first time a productivity supplement for increased efficiency and flexible working practices. The agreement sought to break down Ford's own rigid bureaucratic system of categorising semi-skilled work and also the craft demarcations it had inherited from the history of British craft unionism. Far-reaching changes in working practices were agreed. 500 job titles were reduced to around 50. For example, a new production operator job title replaced 86 previous job titles! Production operators roles were expanded to take on responsibility for indirect tasks such as minor maintenance (e.g. repair of spot-welding guns), seek and repair, self-certification of work, statistical quality control, line feeding, stock-handling, and cleaning their work areas, thus reducing the need for indirect labour. Various craft demarcations were re-analysed with a view to creating two types of craftsman - a mechanical maintenance craftsman and an electrical craftsman. A key goal is the simplification of the production process using principles similar to those used in Just In Time management (JIT). Inventories have been reduced, tool change time also, and the principle of right first time introduced on the shopfloor. Automation has been introduced in welding and paint areas.

Apart from the more efficient utilisation of labour, these changes are justified on the grounds that they generate greater pride in and responsibility for work and increased job interest. Allied to the goals of altering the composition of work was the acceptance that these expanded tasks required a new emphasis on skills training. The key goal of flexibility is to reduce 'idle time' so that time is used more efficiently. Job cycle times have increased. In a sense, the job is, therefore, enriched though the company does not justify the changes in these terms.

> You don't sell it as job enrichment. You justify it in capital terms.

The changes, therefore, would seem to mark a change in the old Fordist paradigm of decomposition and fragmentation of tasks based on scientific management principles of specialisation and the extreme division of labour.

Allied to the changes in work content is Ford's long-term attempt to create a more cooperative relationship with its employees through the Employee Involvement process. The failure of the attempt to introduce quality circles, the labour relations element of the 'After Japan' initiative, led to a more gradual approach to change in this area and the decision to try and carry the unions along with them as other elements of the package were introduced using the vehicle of Employee Involvement. The key here is trust-building, the attempt to substitute existing low-trust relationships with higher trust. In this area change is necessarily a slow process but management is optimistic. As one senior industrial relations manager put it, 'trust is slowly building'. He was careful, though, not to make too grandiose claims:

> It would be naive of us to suggest that we now have a harmonious, sweet, cooperative working situation that we can relax about. But I just do not have the aggravation my predecessor had two or three years ago. I'm not suggesting there aren't any problems anymore. But we're finding ways of resolving almost all of them locally and without stoppages of work.

The structures of Employee Involvement have only, so far, been accepted by salaried staff. The failure of quality circles and their introduction without consultation and acceptance by the unions has led the hourly unions to be more cautious about a formal commitment to Employee Involvement but management is optimistic that a formal involvement is not too far in the future. For the present the principles of Employee Involvement are being introduced by management in the discussion and implementation of the changes following the reorganisation of work agreed in the 1985 agreement, one of the goals of which is trying to involve the hourly-paid worker in local change initiatives, for example, changes in line organisation, machine lay-out, demarcation problems. In this area there have been notable successes such as the ironing out of manufacturing problems relating to new product and the growth of joint action groups attacking quality problems.

Apart from more efficient utilisation of labour, changes have been aimed at promoting greater pride in and responsibility for work and greater job interest among employees. Self-inspection also reduces the need for inspectors. Rationalisation – the workforce was reduced by 25 per cent between 1979 and 1986 – has been accompanied by a tightening up of discipline and work standards and an emphasis on the upholding of agreed procedures. Particular attention has been paid to time and time-use as a measure of efficiency and productivity. Overtime has been reduced and non-productive time has been squeezed, with relaxation and break periods more tightly supervised. A process logic of production means that machine downtime is the major factor to be eliminated from the system in the pursuit of competitiveness. Flexible working practices help in this to the extent that they cut down on old demarcations. The major factor contributing to low U.K. productivity compared to its continental counterpart, according to Ford management, has not been the pace of the line, although it is slightly faster on the continent, but interruptions to its continuous flow.

MANAGERIAL CHANGE - PARTICIPATIVE MANAGEMENT

To understand the magnitude of the change programme undertaken by Ford management during the 1980s we must appreciate the immense weight of tradition which permeates every level of the organisation. Ford's tightly structured organisation had routinised not only manual work but also relations between managerial groups. In this organisational context, innovative capacity was squeezed by the necessities of bureaucratic compliance. Ironically, however, while innovation was the sole prerogative of senior management groups such personnel had achieved their powerful positions by observing - not challenging - the bureaucratic rules which defined their functions. In Fords, changing managerial cultures was a task no less ambitious than challenging the company's deeply-embedded patterns of work organisation and labour relations.

The major change initiative in this area is participative management, a key goal of which is to change managerial attitudes and inflexible organisational structures. Participative management is aimed at breaking down barriers between managerial groups and integrating their efforts, between, for example, manufacturing and product design, a perennial problem in the car industry. The goal here is a more integrated approach to management and much training effort is being aimed at this although it is considered that this is

> a task for a generation [because] we tend to run on very strict functional lines, what we call organisational chimneys

and the various functional groups do not have the same objectives. The different goals of the various functional groups are now to be subsumed under a common approach to quality improvement, based on a 'whole new way of thinking' according to 'an attitude of service' so that all problems are referred to the touchstone of 'being customer-driven'. The company thus becomes more 'business-oriented' rather than, as previously, 'numbers-oriented' and quality becomes the most important plant objective. Once again it is stressed that this process of change can only be

> very slow in the bureaucratic situation which we have [not least] because the people at the top of the organisation got where they are by being successful in the old mould and it comes hardest for them more than for anybody to change.

There are ongoing initiatives towards simplifying Ford's complex management structures and its top-down management style with detailed analysis of all decisions thus making the decision-making process slow and inflexible. Control systems have been simplified to produce a devolution of authority to the level in the organisation at which it is needed. During the course of its history Ford has developed a sophisticated approach to management, based on mass-assembly techniques and complex and elaborate management information systems, operating within a strictly defined line and staff structure. This led to a generally directive, top-down management style, extensive and detailed analysis of decisions, and thus slow and inflexible decision-making and a heavy emphasis on short-term financial criteria. This has led to organisation restructuring designed to broaden spans of control, develop responsibility, increase accountability and create more manageable, more self-contained organisational units. Changes at Dagenham in the Body and Assembly Operations exemplify this trend (British Institute of Management 1985). The number of managerial layers has been reduced from eight to five. Previously the body and assembly operations were organised as two separate plants. Production Managers had no responsibility for service activities which were centralised. The multi-tiered, narrow-span-of-control structure meant that decision making had become increasingly remote from the shop floor. To overcome these defects of the system a new Area Management structure had been introduced creating three 'mini plants' (stamping and body construction, paint, and trim and final assembly), with almost the full range of services and a single Production Manager reporting to each Area Manager. The revised structure provides direct support services for production activities through more manageable units operating as self-contained businesses with improved lines of communication. Responsibility is, thus, significantly devolved with area managers given increased responsibility for all aspects of production, maintenance and quality control.

> The production manager becomes a mini plant manager with total responsibility for doing the job.

The elimination of organisational levels was subsequently extended by the deletion of General Operations manager positions coordinating several operations across Europe and with the elimination of the role of General Foreman and its replacement by fewer, more flexible Senior Foremen who act as assistants to a slightly increased number of Superintendents.

Management style has become a major element of the change agenda with senior Ford executives being trained in a more participative and problem-solving management style. One important example of the changes aimed at in the relationship between managerial groups is the closer integration of design and production engineering to eliminate problems that have arisen in manufacturing in the past due to poor liaison between these groups. This is a particularly important change area at a time of accelerating technological change (Burns and Stalker 1961; Institution of Production Engineers 1980).

Ford's competitive strategy for the future is clearly set out in the 1985 Annual Report:

> To hold its leadership in the U.K. and ensure long-term profitability, Ford has adopted a firm consumer-based strategy. Its purpose is the development of new models which reflect the highest standards in design, technology and innovation, while ensuring that all improvements are based on what the customer really wants. Along with this commitment the Company's highest priority is to make certain that every vehicle from Ford is first in quality for its class.

1985, as well as signalling turnaround in the company's competitive situation, was also a year of major technological advance. Changes introduced in the late 1970s and early 1980s started to show results.

> 1985 was one of the most significant periods of innovation in the Company's 75 year history. Many of the technological developments of recent years were brought to fruition, extending the Ford product range into areas of refinement previously not available in the mass market. (Annual Report, 1985)

Significant innovations in this area were anti-lock braking, electronic engine management systems, four-wheel drive, heated windscreens and advances in 'lean burn' engine technology, leading to improved fuel efficiency and reduced exhaust emission levels. The new emphasis on product quality led to a new role for the quality control function with the new 'conscious and deliberate programme of measurement engineering' (Pettigrew, T.J., 1985, p.87).

A new emphasis on the integration of the management of design, manufacture and marketing highlighted the crucial importance of what Lorenz (1986) calls the 'design dimension'. Of key importance here is the expanded attention paid to the quality function throughout the company. Quality is no longer just part of the production function. The broader understanding of the importance of quality arises from the definition of quality in terms of conformance to customer requirements. This emphasis ensures that the quality assurance process takes in both design and manufacture. By making marketing an integral part of the process too it ensures that the customer's requirements are paramount in the design process. Marketing thus becomes 'a central driving force of corporate strategy' (Lorenz 1986, p.viii).

As we have seen, the movement of marketing to the centre of corporate strategy represents an historic shift of emphasis through which the interests of the customer for the first time superceded the interests of the company. The company moved from a product orientation to a customer orientation. A key element in the return to competitiveness was 'Ford's transformation from design dullard into leader':

> Starting in Europe in the late 1970s, it completely broke away from its traditional strategy of providing worthy but boring products on a narrow sales platform of 'value for money'. ... Instead the entire Ford organization seized on a nascent European trend towards aero-dynamics to leapfrog its competitors. ... In one courageous and risky bound it scrapped the time-honoured Detroit tradition of evolution at a snail's pace, and catapulting itself forward by a generation. (Lorenz 1986, p.90)

Product design and the ability to target specific products at finer market niches became a key competitive weapon (Lorenz 1986, p.3). New computer systems enable the speedier communication of information about market performance between dealers and the company thus facilitating quick reactions to market changes. The changes reflect the importance of the strategy, described by Robert Lutz, of 'moving up in technology and credibility' (quoted Lorenz 1986, p.91).

Design and the quest for quality were combined in the new approach, the first fruit of which was the Sierra. This approach meant a radical change in organisational structures and product development procedures and a new key strategic role for the industrial designer who was integrated into line management as part of the new key focal role in the integration of marketing and engineering. A matrix structure was introduced to integrate the work of product development. This required an extension of the principles of participative management to counter the inertial qualities of functional boundaries. The ability to cross these boundaries and thus attain organisational flexibility has been an important element in Japan's success. In Product Development the same managerial logic that motivated the change to Area Management in Manufacturing has generated changes in component engineering activities. These have been reorganised, eliminating two tiers of structure and establishing units of 7-10 engineers under each supervisor handling a range of related components. Component responsibility is assigned to the supervisor for the whole range, rather than to the engineer for the individual component so that tasks can be assigned as workload demands. This has: increased the breadth of engineers' jobs and, thus, job interest; provided more flexible operations; and improved lateral and vertical communication.

Also important here is the need to change corporate culture so that it is no longer dominated by one functional group. In the car industry this group has tended to be financial with an emphasis on short-term financial returns. An emphasis on the importance of design and marketing –

> the sensitive understanding of various customer groupings, and the design of different products to suit their various preferences. (Lorenz 1986, p.147)

– needs a longer-term, more strategic perspective.

This new perspective is clearly visible in changes in the company's relationships with its suppliers. Improvement in product quality requires not only new, more flexible working practices on the part of the workforce and management but also a different relationship with suppliers. There is better coordination and planning of stock-handling to facilitate the reduction of stock levels that is an important part of a movement towards Just in Time management, one of the elements of 'After Japan'. The company also demands higher standards of quality, reliability and continuity of supply so that it can meet its own quality and inventory targets. It is providing increased assistance to suppliers in achieving these higher standards. Supplier quality assurance is an important new development. Formal groups comprising supplier and Ford personnel such as product and process engineers and quality control technicians have been established. Suppliers are expected to adopt the Ford approach to quality improvement and assurance. The emphasis is on the rationalisation of the supplier network. There are two main reasons for this. Collaboration with suppliers demands time therefore concentration of time and effort on one rather than a number of suppliers is seen as the better quality strategy.

Because, also, the new approach tends to reduce production costs, the policy of single sourcing is seen as being a mutually beneficial method of parts price reduction: better than the present multi-source competitive tendering principle. (Pettigrew, T.J., 1985, pp.87-88)

Traditionally, the relationship between the company and its suppliers has not been one of high trust but, with moves towards more long-term relationships, there is evidence that this key relationship is evolving.

CONCLUSION - THE PROCESS OF CHANGE

At Ford of Britain the managerial response to the new competitive challenges the company faces in the 1980s has centred on the search for new working agreements aiming at the rationalisation and intensification of work allied to a range of initiatives aimed at developing more flexible working practices in production and management. Underlying these changes lies a market strategy geared to product diversity based on a narrower, more precise definition of market segments with an acceleration of the model replacement cycle. The work organisation changes at the shopfloor level involve the long-term renegotiation of the psychological contract between the individual worker and the company through management improving its communication of relevant business information to employees and the fostering of employee involvement, the psychological contract supplementing the formal contract of employment in a positive sense, geared to cooperation rather than control and its inevitable concomitant, conflict. Fordism as a principle of work organisation survives as an emphasis on the right to manage and the payment of high wages based on measured day-work not piece-rates. But Fordism in the sense of the fragmentation and close supervision of work as key guiding managerial principles is in the process of modification with moves towards employee involvement.

Employee involvement aims at introducing more reliability and quality into the production process. U.K. unions' slow take-up of the features that have marked the employee involvement process in the U.S., particularly quality circles, indicates that change in the British context is a long, slow process, needing a different form of management, one that is especially patient in its approach to change, if these initiatives are to be successful in the long-term. The narrowness of the acceptance by the labour force of the conditions of the 1985 pay agreement indicates how slender a margin separates success from failure in key areas of management strategy. There are grounds for optimism. The stress on the binding quality of agreements and the dissemination of the need for efficiency as a response to internal, albeit continental, competition, has started to produce major dividends, as the increasingly efficient performance of Dagenham and, especially, Halewood, for so long a thorn in the company's side as far as labour problems were concerned, testify.

Employee involvement constitutes a long-term investment in the future, as its principles are purposefully introduced in a slow but thoroughly worked out fashion so that they do become, eventually, a deeply sedimented part of company culture, of which they will represent, if successful in their grounding in worker attitudes, a major change of direction in the Ford managerial ethos, rather than a quick fix (Kilmann 1984). Ford has been criticised in the past for its failure to change quickly enough, for example, for its failure to attack demarcations and change working practices. The former Director of Industrial Relations, Paul Roots, has defended the company's cautious approach, pointing out that Ford has always differed in important respects from other car firms, most notably in its profitability, and that the company, therefore, has had less need of dramatic change than have some other firms. In making changes the company is wary of making sudden moves and seeks continued change as part of a considered programme of development (Roots 1986). The failure of the quality circle initiative demonstrates the dangers of approaching change too quickly and ignoring the deep-seated nature of an organisation's way of doing things, built up throughout the years of its history.

Crosby (1979), describing the change process at ITT, maintains that it took up to seven years of unrelenting effort so change the company's culture. Japanese companies needed a decade of training for the new approach to quality to permeate through companies. Only when this had been achieved were quality circles introduced (Lorenz 1981b). Ford now accept that change is a slow process that must be carefully managed.

> We in Ford calculate that it will be five years, maybe ten, before we have the new approach fully understood and all its consequences implanted as normal working practices. We have only made a beginning. Yet the results already achieved are remarkable.
> (Pettigrew, T.J., 1985, p.88)

These results include a progressive reduction in warranty repair rate and cost, a reduction in production costs, and a relative increase in customer satisfaction with Ford cars compared with their competitors. The success of the 1985 pay deal and the improvements the company has been able to achieve in efficiency and product quality indicate how the more cautious approach to change can work.

A key element of the change process has been learning how to manage change. The company accepts that it still had as long way to go. Despite reductions in its workforce by 25 per cent during the 1980s — without compulsory redundancies — redeployment and extensive retraining, the U.K. factories still lag behind their continental counterparts. All U.K. factories were meeting their production schedules by late 1986 but, in terms of hours taken to build a car, they lagged behind the Saarlouis plant in West Germany, claimed to be the most efficient assembly plant in Europe, by some 60 per cent. In the U.K. Ford are still looking for annual productivity improvements of the order of 8 per cent over the next 6 years to narrow the gap with the continental plants which are expected to increase productivity at a rate of 6 per cent per annum. The company expects to get the cost per car in U.K. factories down to the level of the European plants but productivity in terms of car output per man is more problematic.

In terms of the management of the shopfloor the key change at Ford can perhaps be summed up in Walton's (1985) notion of a change from management by control to management by commitment. According to this perspective the company is negotiating its way through a transition from 'a strategy based on imposing control' to 'a strategy based on eliciting commitment' (Walton 1985, p.78). This interpretation of events at Ford is corroborated by Guest (1986), writing of his experiences as a consultant to a Ford U.S. plant. Key work organisation changes have been made to promote efficiency, productivity and quality. These are based on tapping hidden employee potential by developing their commitment to the company. Adopting this labour relations strategy means that training assumes an increasing strategic importance.

The changes necessitate major redefinition of the functions of middle and lower level management and also have implications for the size of the managerial workforce. Guest (1986) argues that Western companies have traditionally been over-supervised. American companies average 12 managerial levels compared with Japanese companies' seven. Also corporate management is chronically under-utilised leaving scope for rationalisation in the office of the same order that has been applied to the shopfloor. The implication of a devolution of authority to the shopfloor further strengthens this tendency. In a labour relations strategy geared to the elicitation of commitment the role of the supervisor becomes pivotal.

> The commitment model requires first-line supervisors to facilitate rather than direct the work force, to impart rather than merely practice their technical and administrative expertise, and to help workers develop the ability to manage themselves. ... The new breed of supervisor must have a level of interpersonal skill and conceptual ability often lacking in the present supervisory work force. (Walton 1985, pp.82-83)

The change in the supervisor's role necessitated by the redesign of work has been demonstrated by Gyllenhammer (1977) in his study of Volvo. He argues that the foreman has to bear the heaviest responsibility for the implementation of change. Crucially, he has to change from being a disciplinarian to a coordinator and motivator of work groups. The foreman's role, therefore, changes from 'task master to communicator between labour and top management' (Giordano 1986, pp.28-29).

The changes also have profound implications for the internal politics of a company. It is crucial, in terms of implementing work organisation changes, that power is invested in those who support such changes. Participative management is based on the principle of a more equitable sharing of power. The development of a capacity for innovation based on the strengthening of as company's design capability requires that more groups gain access to key strategic decision arenas (Whipp and Clark 1986). Participative Management also requires integration between the various managerial functions and, ultimately, a move away from functional to a more general management perspective. This requires a change in traditional organisational cultures, often grounded in functional loyalties, and the development of mechanisms to cultivate integration. The evidence suggests that this form of change is one of the most difficult of all to implement. Kanter (1985), in her study of change at General Motors, wonders whether integration is attainable after years of functional and divisional competition, currently embodied in the 'lead division' concept. A key part of the Ford competitive strategy is comparison between plants, which raises the question of whether a strategy of commitment can co-exist with one of internal competition and what cooperative initiatives might overcome the need for internal competition as a driving force of change.

At General Motors it is the finance functions that tend to dominate corporate strategic decision-making. Ford Europe has recently seen the replacement as Chairman of Bob Lutz, 'a car "buff" who enjoys getting deeply involved in product development', with Kenneth Whipple whose core expertise is finance (Financial Times, 6 May 1987) which might be construed as not auguring well for the development of the innovatory approach to corporate strategy and as marking a swing back to too restricted an emphasis on efficiency. Part of the 'After Japan' campaign was the development of central control over quality, cost and breakeven standards and the establishment of more rigorous and more sophisticated cost control systems (Marsden, Morris, Willman and Wood 1986). The work of Abernathy demonstrates how difficult a knife-edge the balance between innovation and productivity is to negotiate. Ford suffered in the past under Henry Ford II when finance specialists with little knowledge of the strategic importance of product development, were introduced to implement much-needed financial controls. These specialists came to dominate company decision-making. The tight financial controls they introduced inhibited product development, the production function suffered as plant became increasingly obsolescent, and the company ended up with bigger and bigger cars, ripe for the Japanese challenge (Halberstam 1987).

Major changes in work organisation have seen the reduction of unit labour costs as well as moves towards a more flexible workforce. Roots highlights the importance of pay bargaining in the change process and how pay increases are not incompatible with the control of labour costs.

A further key area is pay bargaining. Many politicians and economists are surprised that, despite high unemployment and falling inflation, wage settlements have continued to run at a high level. That is because they do not understand that employers are interested not in wage rates, but in labour costs. Firms are willing to grant wage increases if the labour costs do not go up. Although unit labour costs may not be falling as fast as some people might wish, they are certainly falling, and if you think about all the de-manning that has been going on, you will realise that the average company has a very rapidly falling wage bill. In addition, labour costs in many companies are not such a significant feature of total production costs as they previously were because with the use of more technology and the restructuring of work companies are making savings on their overheads. For example, by raising quality levels they are cutting scrap costs. In this atmosphere, employers are not keen to risk a strike to cut wage increases. When the CBI [Confederation of British Industry] and the government say that we have to reduce the level of wage settlements they are missing the point. It is not wage levels that we have to reduce; it is our total manufacturing costs. Employers are, moreover, prepared to take things at a certain pace in order to maintain the cooperation of their workers with the changes they are making. (Roots 1986, p.7)

Ford management is in the process of critically re-examining some of its deepest assumptions, even expressing a willingness to consider the central plank of its measured day-work pay policy in the light of the potential earnings advantage of Austin Rover's bonus system if earnings differentials should ever grow too great. We are seeing a change in the industrial relations function in line with the image of the future shape of work in the company as human factors assume a growing importance.

The trouble-shooting and fire-fighting elements of the industrial relations function are declining, and we are playing an increasing role in general planning. Management is increasingly recognising the importance of people, and personnel specialists are being called in by other managers at an earlier stage. There is in Ford a growing emphasis on workers as people. (Roots 1986, p.7)

It is important to emphasise, though, that there has been no abrogation of the 'right to manage'. Indeed, this principle has been been re-affirmed with the emphasis the company has given to the enforcement of agreements. But there is certainly a change of emphasis in the industrial relations climate. The emphasis on new skills to generate the kind of workforce that current changes are geared to has meant a growing importance for the company's training program and the communication of information about the company's competitive position to the workforce. Particular importance was attached to the need to disseminate information about the threat posed by Nissan in the North-East. The industrial relations function, thus, assumes a growing importance in corporate planning.

The work organisation changes currently underway at Ford indicate a transition to a new form of employment contract based on a more generally skilled workforce. Production workers are experiencing some expansion of their roles with a reduction in the fragmentation that previously characterised their work and, in the craft sphere, old demarcations are being whittled away as new technologies demand redefinition of skill boundaries and retraining. Thus there are moves towards flexibility in job definition and consequent changes in wage structures. The indications are that the unions are accepting the need/inevitability of these changes. The 1985 pay deal marks a major step forward in this direction. The key to the continuing success of the company's change initiatives is the extent to which the acceptance of the need for change can continue to be built upon. Two major sources of optimism for the future would seem to be Employee

40

Involvement and Participative Management. A key factor in the Employee Involvement process will be the degree to which acceptance of it can be gained on the shopfloor. The quest for more Participative Management as a strategy for institutionalising the acceptance of the need to carry the change process forward reminds us, however, that change needs to permeate the whole company not just one of its layers.

Despite major gains in productivity, efficiency and quality improvements, the company still argues that it is the early stages of transformation, that 'the mountain is still up there ahead of us'. However, its assessment of its current situation is marked by a cautious optimism demonstrated in the decision of early 1987 to expand capacity in British plants, to expand the British content of cars made here, and, later this decade, to start exporting cars from Britain again, a decision that reflects a growing trust on management's part in the productive capacity of the British workforce. The change process would seem, therefore, to be moving in a direction that meets senior Ford management approval despite the undoubted problems the company still faces.

For those managers involved in the implementation of change the experience can be frustrating. As one employee relations manager explained, he had a sense of progressing

two steps forward, one step backwards.

Backward movement is attributed to inevitable mistakes on management's part as it learns to facilitate change. These mistakes hinder the nurturing of trust relationships. It is the lack of trust that is the major barrier to change. Some managers see the change agent role of the external consultants working on the Employee Involvement/ Participative Management process as crucial in developing trust.

There are still the 35 years of traditional conflict which doesn't exactly enhance trust. The third party, the ability to have that intervention, is, without question, critical in the establishment of the process and key in its continuation.

Initial enthusiasms generated by the 'After Japan' campaign have been tempered by the realisation of the difficulties of the change process and the necessity of progress being based on

compromise between the old ways and something a bit more participative.

Employee Involvement is very much in its early days and is not seen as a panacea.

You have to accept the disappointment and the frustration and the time it takes. You've got to be incredibly patient.

Some managers favour a non-formal approach as the most productive way of implementing change:

approaching normal business in a participative sort of way, taking the opportunities that present themselves, as the Americans say, 'Doing it where you can' and 'Doing what feels good'. If you stick to that approach then you will gradually, not in a very radical sort of way, gradually infuse a more participative philosophy. Given the cynical, resistant nature of the British people, that's probably the best way of making progress.

The formal structures, according to this point of view, are not as important as the 'whole stylistic, philosophical thing'.

Problem-solving workgroups are not what involvement is all about. Maybe you need the problem-solving workgroups to teach people to do it, to build it into the philosophy, but unless it becomes a normal way of doing business ... they ought in theory to go away.

The changes currently underway do seem to mark a major change in the company philosophy of employee relations. One senior industrial relations manager encapsulated the change of emphasis:

The industrial relations fraternity is starting to ask itself questions like 'Are we policemen or are we supposed to be innovators in terms of creating a work climate in which people can fulfil their own ambitions and gain self-awareness?' In a twenty year career in industrial relations in Ford Motor Company I haven't heard that sort of question until the last 18 months. 'Are we policemen or innovators?'.

Of course, the change in the economic climate in Britain has been instrumental in introducing the awareness of the need for change and acceptance of change measures. This gives rise to the question whether change would have been possible without the economic pressures and the threats hanging over the future of Ford in Britain. Ford management see the changes as certainly being influenced by this factor:

It's awful to have to say it, one tries to convince oneself that it's the purity of the change process that turns people on, but to get change you [may have to] confront them with a potential disaster.

But at the same time new skills were necessary to navigate the company through what appears to be a major transition period. As one manager deeply involved with the Employee Involvement process expressed it:

It was the potential disaster together with new skills that enabled the transformation to take place. It was neither one nor the other that led to the change.

3 Pilkington Brothers

INTRODUCTION

Pilkington Brothers is one of the world's largest producers of glass and related products. Founded in 1826 as the St. Helens Crown Glass Company, its headquarters remain on the original St. Helens site. The company remained a dynastic organisation until 1970 when it went public to enable further expansion in an increasingly capital intensive industry. Nevertheless, despite public flotation, Pilkington's current chairman is Sir Antony Pilkington, the sixth family chairman.

Family domination and concentration in a - historically - largely single-industry town combined to create a strongly paternalistic ethos within the company, an ethos which pervaded not only labour relations but also a gentlemanly disdain for aggressive marketing and a heavy reliance on technical excellence. In this chapter we shall examine how the company reacted to fierce challenges in its core markets by strategic realignment, work reorganisation and cultural change. The distinctive feature of the change process in Pilkington is the company's reliance on existing managerial expertise in setting the change agenda. In this sense, Pilkington can be described as a case study in a typical British approach to organisational change, based on pragmatism and learning through experience.

PILKINGTON BROTHERS

Even the most cursory examination of the businesses under the corporate umbrella of the Pilkington Brothers Group reveals that the organisation is much more than a single-product, glassmaking firm. Currently, Pilkington Brothers Group operations are organized in six product divisions, with central headquarter's providing Group services, Group Research and Development, and Group Engineering functions. The Group operates from 12 principal manufacturing locations in the United Kingdom and has more than 20 subsidiary and related companies in the United Kingdom and 30 in overseas countries. The Group's principal activities are the manufacture, processing and marketing of products which include: flat glass; glass fibre reinforcement material, a substitute for asbestos in building products; opthalmic glass such as fast-reacting photochromic glass, high-performance coated glass; safety glass, for example, high-strength glass for architectural, automobile and aircraft usage; a large variety of products combining optics and electronics for, primarily, electro-optical medical and defence applications; pressed and extruded glass; and plastics for the building, automobile, communications and furniture industries. The company holds a world-wide reputation for process and product innovation which include: the float glass process, the universal method for manufacturing high quality flat glass and a paradigmatic case of successful technological innovation; triplex high strength glass; alkali resistant glass fibre; and photochromic lenses.

In the post-1945 era Pilkington's strength has been derived from product and process innovation. In particular, the invention of the 'float processes' which revolutionised flat glassmaking (Barker 1977). By floating a continuous ribbon of molten glass on a bed of molten tin this process markedly improved the optical quality and versatility of the glass. Prior to the float glass process, conceived and developed between 1952 and 1959, glassmaking had been a highly labour-intensive process of grinding and polishing. While the initial justification for the development of the float process had been reduced operating costs in fact it enabled the production of higher quality glass at the same cost. Pilkington was faced by a predicament by this innovation. The company could not monopolise the process nor use it to compete outside its established domestic and Empire markets without sparking a long-term price and technology war. Given the enormous development costs entailed during the decade of development and the unappetising prospect of a worldwide trade war Pilkington decided on marketing the new technology through international licensing. By 1969 all the world's major glass manufacturers had taken licenses for the process (Ryan 1984). Pilkington have used the royalty and licence income raised between 1960 and 1987 to finance ongoing product development. The licencing of the float process in this way stabilised the world glass industry into a series of national markets dominated by highly capital-intensive firms. For Pilkington, a further beneficial consequence of licencing was that it cemented long-term relationships with its competitors which gave the company access to further incremental process and product innovations. Less positively, the success of licensing confirmed the organisation's primary orientation as being technology rather than market-driven.

For over a century Pilkington was synonymous with company paternalism, the myriad welfare provisions through which the company strove to consolidate its authority both inside its factories and in the local community. From 1945 the increasing scale of glass production and the diversification of the economic life of St. Helens gradually loosened the age-old ties between employer and employee. A bitter seven week wildcat strike in 1970 was to prove a watershed in Pilkington's industrial relations development (Lane and Roberts 1971). In effect, the 1970 strike was a clash between the past and the present which neither a paternalist management nor a highly centralised collective bargaining structure could contain. The dispute was not, however, an unambiguous conflict between antiquarian management practices and a modern, 'instrumental' workforce whose loyalty to the firm could no longer be guaranteed through company welfare provisions. Rather, an underlying theme to the dispute was the workforce's ambivalence about the passing of the old paternalist regime and the increasing remoteness of senior management and trade unionism from the daily realities of shopfloor life. As we shall see, if the 1970 strike dismantled the old paternalist structure of authority within Pilkington's it was to take the equally traumatic business experience of the late-seventies recession to finally decentralise collective bargaining. Decentralisation effectively eliminated this problem by making the business performance of the individual plant and division the yardstick for collective bargaining, not the fortunes of the Pilkington Group as a whole.

PRESSURES FOR CHANGE

The Company entered the 1980s with a growing number of problems. The oil shocks of the 1970s had immense implications for the energy intensive glassmakers and upset the informal observation of the first rule of the world glass industry; non-intervention in the core national markets of the major British, French, American and Japanese players. The European 'glass wars' had a dramatic impact on Pilkington's market position; its privileged position of near monopoly of the domestic market was drastically eroded by import penetration. By the close of the decade Pilkington's market share had dropped from a high of 80 per cent to 50 per cent of the U.K. glass business. It was also experiencing production cost problems associated with inefficient and non-competitive working practices. 1980-82 saw two years of steady losses in the U.K. As a result, the years since have been a time of transformation in strategy, structure, culture and working practices.

The last four years have been ones of great change, necessitating difficult and sometimes painful readjustment. (Chairman's Statement, Annual Report 1985)

Readjustment was necessary to meet changing market conditions and, also, because the company had lost the technological edge it once enjoyed. Changes in working practices were needed to make the most efficient use of a technology it shares with its major competitors.

Pilkington's problems reflected those of the British economy generally in a time of acute recession. Antony Pilkington, the Chairman since 1982, singled out, as the 'two most obvious external forces which have influenced the rate of change', the continuing decline of the British motor industry and the sudden and unexpected loss of Government financial support for council house loft insulation. (Annual Report, 1985)

In addition, the licencing of the float glass process which generated the revenues necessary to finance research and development began to elapse. Between 1981-84, eleven licences expired – covering forty eight plants, nearly 75 per cent of Pilkington's licencing income (Ryan 1984, p.4). The effects of the transformations in strategy, structure, culture and working practices are still working their way through the Company but are already reflected in significant steps back to competitiveness.

ACHIEVING CHANGE

In the 1980s there has been a major reshaping of the Group both through acquisition of companies pioneering emergent electro-optical technologies and internal reorganisation. This saw major changes of strategic direction in the diversification away from traditional products and markets and geographical diversification most notably into the US with the acquisition of a 30 per cent holding in the Libbey-Owens-Ford Company, a diversified manufacturer of glass and plastic products, fluid power and fluid system components. This acquisition provided Pilkington's with a major trading platform in a country where it had not previously had any major interests and an important stake in the US automobile and construction industries. There was diversification in its insulation operations into low temperature range products giving it a complete range of low to high temperature insulation products and a parallel divestment of operations now considered unviable such as some elements of its reinforcements glass business. Finally, there were important developments in the 'downstream' side of the glass business with a new emphasis on value-added products as opposed to the previous concentration on flat glass. The importance of downstream diversification is evidenced by the company's stated intention of trebling such activities so that they will comprise one third of Group business by 1990.

Structural changes saw a major rationalisation of the company's divisional structure with the merging of the Flat Glass and the Safety Glass divisions into a single division, Pilkington Glass Division. Previously the company had distinguished between glass supplied to the building industry and glass supplied to the motor industry, supplying each from the separate divisions. The company had found a growing overlap between the divisions, for example, in the new emphasis being placed on safety glass in building legislation. This led to an overlap of technology, product and market. Hence rationalisation under a single divisional structure and the creation of a division manufacturing both raw unprocessed and processed glass. The new division was, therefore, responsible for the capital intensive and continuous processing of the raw product and for the manufacture of the growing number of higher value added products with a new structure to generate economies of scale and simplify the managerial process.

The years since 1983 have seen a slow but steady improvement in trading performance with U.K. operations returning to profit for the first time in 1984 since the losses of the early 1980s. This has been offset by the high redundancy and pension make-up costs that the Company took on as part of its radical restructuring of the workforce. An accelerated write-off of these costs over a three-year period was initiated in 1984. The improved results of 1983–84 reflect the first effects of initial steps in cost reduction and productivity gains in traditional manufacturing areas due to rationalisation and manpower reduction, cost cutting, and strict capital expenditure controls. This was achieved despite overcapacity in the industry, strong competition and the continuing depressed state of the building industry and the British car industry. Between 1981–85 around 7000 jobs had been shed while output per man increased by 7 per cent, against a background of almost static sales in both the building and motor industries. Pilkington's core businesses improved their cost structures, despite the continuing problems of low margins in processed glass in the auto and building industries. In all business areas manufacturing capacity was better matched to market demand. The focus of attention throughout the company was now on improving plant yields, plant utilisation, and margins in highly competitive market environments. By 1986 all Pilkington's U.K. divisions had returned to profit.

1985 also witnessed a major restructuring of strategic level responsibilities. Operational and profit responsibility for budgeting, manufacturing, marketing, dividend policies and industrial relations was delegated to divisional Chief Executives. Prior to this each board member was also a divisional chairman, an arrangement which generated conflicting loyalties and hindered the development of long-term strategic objectives for the Group as a whole. Divisional innovations in product or process must now find a sponsoring director through whom a chief executive can lobby the board or hear its thinking on capital spending or new policy directions (<u>Financial Times</u>, 12 June 1985). Much of the Group's highly elaborate central committee structure was dismantled and decisions devolved to the operational level. Divisional reliance on the centre was minimised and wage bargaining decentralised. The structure of the board itself was radically changed with the reallocation of responsibilities and the reduction of the number of executive directors from ten to seven while retaining the five non-executive directors. Strategic level reorganisation represented the culmination of a change process in which a central strand was to increase managerial responsibility for operating decisions and focus worker attention on plant, rather than corporate, performance as the touchstone to job security and pay settlements.

A key element of the change process was the need for a change in managerial culture. Pilkington had a long-established reputation for technical excellence. This was now to be allied to the same 'slow but intense' introduction of change in working practices. The goal was the improvement of performance and efficiency which, by comparison with non-United Kingdom installations, was poor, against a background of recession and deteriorating company performance. The company had to come to terms with the reality of competition and the fact that the Group no longer held the privileged position of 'huge main suppliers to 80 per cent of the market' as market share steadily deteriorated.

In terms of strategic direction the company 'has moved away from the base that it had' into new markets, becoming much more market-sensitive:

> there is no question [now] that the company is very sensitive to the need to develop an understanding of the customer. Pressure on markets, pressure on prices, that's been the driving force that's driven the divisions to worry a hell of a lot more about the customer. [For example] we put a plant in Corby to sell to the market down there. We would never have thought about that 10, 20 years ago. [We've taken] many more strategic decisions because of the market situation ... driven by the need to get back to where we were.

In turn, the organisation has had to become much more flexible to react quickly to customer requirements.

> Customer response in the market place so the customer can get right in there and get delivery within 24 hours. Systems have been developed in order to do that. We can deliver literally within 24 hours. That was never contemplated some years ago. Fibre-glass, 24 hours for the customer on their doorstep. They've really had to jump to match customer requirements.

The importance of this new stress on commercial and manufacturing excellence should not be under-estimated. Pilkington's long-held market dominance had embedded the concern for technical excellence deep within the Pilkington managerial psyche. Pilkington managers recount tales of the search for technical excellence which ran counter to plant efficiency and testified to an almost willful disdain for customer needs. The commercial folly of such attitudes was made abundantly clear in the harsh trading environment of the late-seventies. For Group chairman, Antony Pilkington, cultural change – reversing the imbalance between technical and commercial expertise – was a paramount competitive priority for the 1980s and beyond. Above all, this involved forcing plant managers whose status within the company had been ascribed according to the complexity of the plant they managed, to accept commercial – rather than simply production – responsibilities. Pilkington was fortunate that it had established a capacity for self-analysis, having learned from its long involvement with consultants from Manchester Business School, particularly in the area of productivity bargaining, to think in terms of a systems approach to its functioning and problems. Antony Pilkington communicated the difficult lessons learnt through self-analysis:

> Now the only way to get an edge on the competition is to emphasise the marketing end. But that is easier said than done if you have a company with a long tradition that based its success on operating complex plants. We almost need to grow a new breed of person. (Financial Times, 12 June 1985)

The quotation is redolent with meaning. Plant management can no longer be simply a matter of 'operating' complex process technologies but requires marketing competence. Equally significant is the explicit recognition of the need for slow, organic change because technical excellence and centralism have been central, defining characteristics of Pilkington culture for so long. The question, then, is how have Pilkington attempted to balance the necessity of slow change with the urgency of rapid improvements in productivity and marketing imposed by the company's deteriorating market position?

REORGANISING WORK

The background to changes in working practices at Pilkington was a growing awareness of the poor efficiency record of its British plants compared with similar plants producing similar products abroad. Pilkington's international licensing arrangements for the float glass process permitted the company access to comparative data on the widening efficiency gap between itself and other major glassmakers. It was the knowledge of this widening gap and its increasing market importance which prompted the decision to invest in the latest technology in a greenfield site at Greengate, St. Helens, in 1981. Greengate provided the opportunity to demonstrate that Pilkington's was capable of matching the best practices of its competitors, of reversing the company's dwindling competitiveness in a sector plagued by massive overcapacity.

The Board was saying: 'We can demonstrate. We must match the best practices'.

It was a crucial first step in the search for efficiency and productivity throughout the company.

Productivity because you can't get the prices down. We had to lower our costs, hence the need for restructuring. It wasn't just a personnel issue. There was an absolute business need there.

Pilkington opened its new float glass factory at Greengate in April 1981. This has 404 employees and produces 5,000 tonnes a week. The old sheet glass plant needed 680 employees to produce 1,800 tonnes a week. A major factor in these productivity gains was that in the new factory the company insisted on new working practices, negotiating arrangements and pay and conditions that were substantially different form those operating in its other factories. This 'personnel package'

was designed to avoid a range of problems which management believes exist at other Pilkington plants – high staffing levels, strict job demarcations, high levels of absenteeism, and complex pay structures involving various premiums and allowances. (IDS Study 312, 1984, p.26)

A key enabling principle introduced at Greengate was that of harmonisation. Staff and factory workers were to have the same conditions of service, a monthly salary and a common pay structure. According to this structure, which was based on job evaluations performed by external management consultants, 53 jobs were divided into ten grades. There was also harmonisation of hours of work and an end to overtime payments. Additional hours worked entitled the worker to hours off in lieu. Despite the absence of premium payments for overtime working, pay is higher at Greengate than at other Group factories. Staff status and higher wages were awarded in return for the extra job flexibility built into the Greengate working arrangements. Manning at Greengate is tighter and more flexible than in the rest of the Group's operations. At other plants there would be several kinds of jobs in one area, such as the furnace. At Greengate the batch plant operating, melting and forming tasks are amalgamated into one 'glassmaking operator' role.

> The warehouse operation takes the ribbon glass and cuts and stacks it. Traditionally this area would include machine minders, examiners, forklift operators, crane drivers and sweepers ... these have been combined into one operator post. The same has been done in the stock area. The whole Greengate manufacturing process is thus covered by only three grades of operator. In fact, flexibility extends beyond this as occasionally operators may be used in areas other than the one in which they are accustomed to work. Warehouse staff may be used in the furnace area. (IDS Study 312, 1984, p.27)

Flexible working was also introduced in the engineering maintenance function where there are now only two craft jobs – mechanical craftsman and electrical craftsman. There are four workers in the engineering maintenance shift teams – an engineering technician, an electrical craftsman, a mechanical craftsman and a service operator responsible for specific items of plant and equipment. The mechanical craftsman attends to fitting, machining, plumbing, welding and blacksmithing. The electrical craftsman deals with the whole range of electrical and electronic equipment in the plant. Both do their own labouring work although they can request the assistance of process workers.

The setting-up of the Greengate operation also involved a searching look at ways of organising time and experimentation with a variety of shift systems, most notably 'five-set' and 'six-set' patterns. Glassmaking is a continuous process. The furnaces are only shut down for major overhauls so work has to be organized to provide continuous round-the-shifts. A combination of the reduction in the length of the working week, attempts to control the amount of overtime worked and the need for improved productivity and greater flexibility necessitated a move away from traditional four crew, three shift patterns. Pilkington had a wide experience of a number of different shift work rotas at float glass plants in the U.K. and overseas on which to base their planned changes in this area and used these to design the system in a way which reduced costs and encouraged self management. The objectives embodied in the new shift arrangements were described by management as follows:

> 1. To provide the right type of people, in the right numbers, at the right time, to meet departmental workloads.
> 2. To provide effective cover for both planned and unplanned absences.
> 3. To give both individuals and teams responsibility for smooth, efficient operation in their section.

4. To allow day-to-day operation with minimal involvement from supervision.
5. To inconvenience employees if there is excessive absence.
6. To limit 'alternative hours' working to a mutually acceptable level (on a site with no paid overtime).
7. To provide working arrangements that are generally acceptable to employees. (IDS Report 461, 1985, p.28.)

A five-set system is worked in the glass-making area. It differs from a four-set pattern in that the fifth crew are explicitly rostered in a cover capacity. For Pilkington this system is ideally suited to the predictable workloads of glassmaking and enables the cover team to perform ancillary work around the plant and to step in for planned and unplanned absences. A similar self-management rationale underpins the six-set system which operates where only one person works at a time, such as the engineering shift teams and quality control technicians, and there must always be cover. Employees in these groups are expected to cover each other. This pattern requires groups of six 'who are all motivated in the same way'. It has the following advantages:

pressure on individuals and teams to operate efficiently; no need for supervisory involvement; flexibility to use day turns and make-up days to provide extra staff if this is appropriate to the workload, otherwise cover is spread evenly; the system caters easily for further reductions in the working week and gives employees considerable flexibility. (IDS Study 312, 1984, p.29)

The intermeshing of the various work teams through the five- and six-set systems was designed to encourage self-management and the sense of team responsibility through the requirement that the various teams are responsible for providing cover for each other. In a very real sense the work teams police their own time use. Disadvantages of the four-set pattern are that it means cover is provided inflexibly when none is actually required and that sickness absence does not inconvenience other shift members so no responsibility for possible effects on other workers is felt by the absentee. It also requires considerable overtime to cover absences. Differences in attitudes to absenteeism under the different shift systems is reflected in the levels of sickness absence: 4.2 per cent under the four-set system, 0.9 per cent under the five-set, and 1.5 per cent under the six-set (British Institute of Management, 1985).

An essential element of the installation of best practice working arrangements at Greengate was the decentralisation of collective bargaining. In its traditional operations Pilkington had had a 'tremendous reputation for being a very centralistic company'. For Pilkington's senior management the Greengate development offered the opportunity to shatter this traditional reliance on centralised decision-making by decentralising collective bargaining to the plant level. Indeed, the new working practices to be introduced at Greengate could not be fitted into a central bargaining mould; Pilkington's senior management were determined that bargaining would not be constricted by references to manning levels at established plants. After Greengate, the touchstone of all negotiations was not a national agreement agreed by Pilkington Group and national unions but the needs of particular sectors of the business analysed and responded to at the local level. So, for instance, Triplex, the manufacturer of safety glass based its negotiations on the health of its principal customer, the automobile industry, and not central management or union fiat. For the Pilkington board the changes were associated with more realistic responses to market situations interpreted at the appropriate local level and also a different managerial culture,

a different style of management, one in which the ball is pushed right down [so that divisional managers became] more accountable and responsible.

Of course, it is one thing to alter the structure of collective bargaining, it is quite another to change deeply entrenched management and worker attitudes. This is particularly true when core organisational values are challenged by an attempt to simultaneously shift loyalties from the Pilkington Group to the particular plant and increase the business awareness of management and workers.

The decentralisation of wage bargaining assumed tremendous significance for the company and is symbolic of the enormous importance it attached to the decentralisation of decision-making in general. Managerial decentralisation and localised bargaining were aimed at lower pay settlements reflecting particular business conditions, and, equally important, 'managing differently'. Personnel directors in the various divisions were being offered 'a unique opportunity to make fundamental changes' by negotiating according to their own particular market needs which were to be explained to their workforces in terms of that particular division's market position and not Pilkington Group's generally. The directive to divisional management from the board was:

you can argue what your business needs are in terms of what you practise in manning. You'll be talking about your business, not just as a part of something bigger, but as something that is total and, so, you can get quite major changes. And you ought to be reflecting the sort of changes we made at Greengate.

The intention was 'to break the culture thing they've had for years' – the recourse to the centre to solve all divisional problems and the reliance on central initiatives. There was a communion of views on this approach between the board and key groups of a new breed of divisional managers who were beginning to think of personnel issues in terms of overall business strategy. Senior divisional managers were, in effect, demanding a new kind of authority in dealing with personnel policy, an authority independent of their relationship with the Pilkington Group.

Well, I've got to negotiate, I will negotiate with my people. They must see me as the paymaster. I can't manage this operation when my people see Pilkington as the paymaster. They must see Pilkington Insulation or Pilkington Glass as the business entity. I must have that total responsibility.

Resistance came from two sources: from some managers who could not
initially 'visualise how they would do it', and from the unions.
Despite prolonged negotiation and management's strong desire to
negotiate the introduction of the new bargaining processes, union
resistance remained strong so that, ultimately, in 1983,
decentralisation of bargaining was imposed unilaterally over the
unions' heads. An unintended consequence and major benefit of the
prolonged negotiation and communication process involved in the
attempt to arrive at agreement was that the understanding of the need
for and acceptance of decentralisation spread, 'so that when it came
to the crunch and there were all sorts of votes about whether to
oppose it or take industrial action, it all fell to the ground' and
the workforce, despite unions advice to the contrary, accepted the
principle. The main union argument against decentralisation had been
that it was a policy aimed at 'divide and rule'. For management, the
workforce were faced with a stark choice between acceptance or further
redundancies; this was an atmosphere in which safeguarding union
prerogatives came second to protecting jobs.

Throughout Pilkington, shop stewards at site level assumed
responsibility for actual negotiations of the new bargaining
arrangements.

I think they liked it. They were having to face up to what had
been agreed and they had to be responsible for that. We saw a
different responsibility coming, I think it's fair to say, a new
responsibility.

Line managers were key agents in the implementation process. Personnel
directors assumed the role of advisers, providing an enabling
function, rather than a directive, industrial relations function.
Greengate proved to be almost four times as efficient as any other
Pilkington glass plant. For senior management, the key to these
productivity gains was not primarily technological but the
introduction of new working practices based on fewer, more flexible
job descriptions. And yet, Greengate remained exceptional within
Pilkington. The key question now facing senior management was: could
the principles behind Greengate be diffused throughout the company's
factories, including those which were long-established?

DIFFUSING CHANGE

Following the success of Greengate work was rationalised and
restructured throughout the company. At the heart of the traditional
areas of the business the St. Helens' labour force was halved between
1979 and 1986. This rationalisation was achieved without compulsory
redundancy and at a pace which did not entirely please the company's
bankers. The length of time the company committed to the process
reflected its respect for the deeply embedded company culture and the
concern with building a platform for ongoing change. Time was needed
to establish a process which would be of use in the future and not
just on a 'one off' basis. The aim was to cultivate a culture of
greater involvement. This involved changing the traditional industrial
relations culture in line with decentralisation. The new working

practices, pioneered at Greengate, were diffused throughout the company by a lengthy participative process of job analysis using the job evaluation methods of a leading firm of management consultants. Again, although the unions opposed the principle of skill flexibility, the workforce accepted its implementation as a necessary trade-off for enhanced job security.

The effects of this broader work reorganisation can be clearly seen in the experiences of the Pilkington Insulation Division, particularly at the Ravenhead plant on which we shall concentrate. The new working practices introduced at Pilkington Insulation's Ravenhead plant were very similar to those introduced at Greengate. What was exceptional at Ravenhead was the introduction of practices pioneered at a greenfield site into a 'brownfield' site - the diffusion of agreements associated with a greenfield site into a long established factory with traditional working arrangements, bargaining practices and payment systems.

The stimulus for change in Pilkington Insulation was a sharp deterioration in the company's trading environment. Pilkington Insulation Division's business is overwhelmingly a U.K. business. The business is strongly affected, therefore, by the vagaries of the U.K. economy. Throughout the 1960s and 1970s the insulation market experienced exponential growth, fuelled by energy conservation drives by successive governments in the wake of escalating oil prices after 1974. Pilkington dominated a sector characterised by under-capacity and reaped high profits from its 60 per cent market share. Inevitably, new entrants arrived in the marketplace, competitors with the advantage of low cost structures based on new plant.

But, nevertheless, if you take it to the end of the '70s, things were still very fat in the insulation business.

In 1980, there was complete change around - 'the world went mad'. The effects of oil price stabilisation and the deepening recession were exacerbated by a radical change in government policy affecting the insulation market. With the success of a Conservative government in the 1979 general election the attitude to the public financing of energy conservation changed. Interventionism gave way to market forces as grant aid for home insulation was reduced. The resulting slump in demand and the presence of new competitors with new, costly capital investments to realise massively intensified competition. The downward pressure on prices and profits was reflected in Pilkington's financial performance. In 1979-80 the division almost doubled its annual profits over the previous year to £20 million. Over the next 18 months it plunged to catastrophic losses of £12 million.

For management, the first task was drastic cost reduction.

Our three major costs are energy, raw materials and labour. You can obviously make savings in energy and raw materials but the scope is fairly limited, whereas the scope for savings in labour was very high. ... The fat times of the 1970s had bred overmanning to a large extent and a fairly soft approach. ... There was extensive demarcation. Just a taste of that - in the craft area there were large numbers of different mechanical trades, without flexibility between them, for example, we had fitters, plumbers, turners, sheet-metal workers, welders, pipe-fitters, and none of them overlapped in any real sense. ... We had tradesmen's labourers carrying craftsmen's bags, the sort of thing you would see, or would have seen, in any other long-standing, highly-unionised North-West industry.

Three main measures were taken to reduce manufacturing costs — capital investment to transfer manually intensive processes onto continuous process lines and investment in automatic handling technology, reducing capacity in line with the level of demand.

In other words, taking capacity out, taking products out that were uneconomical and reducing the numbers employed.

At Ravenhead works these measures halved employee numbers from 1800 to 900 in just over three years. The major reduction was in unskilled process workers. Despite the scale of these manpower reductions they were achieved by voluntary redundancy.

However, Pilkington's efforts to stabilise prices while maintaining market share by reducing manufacturing costs did not solve the division's problems.

The problem wasn't just getting our capacity and costs down. The process 1980-1983 didn't give us anything like the benefits it should have because we were slowly losing market share. We had continued, between 1980 and 1983, to hold onto a leadership posture and to try and maintain prices high through marketing quality and service. We tried to minimise the conflict in the industry so that everybody didn't damage each other through a price competition spiral. We'd tried to lead the price up, or, at least ... keep the price stable, rather than allow it to drift down with competitive pressures. That, in terms of market share, had signally failed because our market share fell during that period from around 60 per cent down to just over 40 per cent, caused by the new competition establishing a position in the market, but also by competition generally exploiting the new market conditions to get share because we were artificially trying to hold onto a high price leadership posture.

1983 witnessed a reversal of this marketing policy and the adoption of a novel, aggressive price cutting policy:

from 1983 onwards we got into the boxing ring on price which we'd not really done in any significant sense before.

During the following unrestricted price war prices tumbled some 30 per cent within six months. Such market brinkmanship was a traumatic experience for a high asset industry with enormous fixed costs. Ultimately, prices stabilised at around 25 per cent below their 1982 level, the point at which there was no longer a market share premium to be gained from continuing the downward spiral of prices. The key issue became, as one senior Pilkington manager explained, which of us could actually stand the pain best, which of us could adapt best to permananently lower revenues from the product we made. Well, unfortunately, despite all the work we'd done, it wasn't us, because, despite halving our numbers at Ravenhead, our sales revenue per employee was £35,000 per year and our new competitors' sales revenue per employee was between £55,000 and £65,000. ... It was very clear that despite all we'd done in productivity terms we were a long, long way behind.

The company's problems can be summarised as: static-to-declining market demand with no possibility of generating a bigger market; unrelenting pressure on prices so that 'to actually go for more market share in an aggressive way was really just re-stimulating the price spiral'; it had already pruned costs through rationalisation but still lagged behind competitors in productivity terms. For senior Insulation management, there was little choice but to adopt

a much more fundamental approach to people costs - structural solutions in other words, rather than simple trimming solutions.

The decision by Pilkington Group to decentralise collective bargaining offered a window of opportunity for just such a radical restructuring of work organisation.

That was an enormous opportunity because ... the inertia, the barriers to changing working practices caused by central negotiations was, for us, enormous because it focussed people on Group norms, the lowest common denominator. An attempt to achieve the needs of specific businesses by a global solution was inappropriate and would have been impossible to engineer. So, putting together the need for a fundamental approach and the opportunity, the team at Ravenhead decided to mount a major restructuring of jobs, working practices and rewards.

The Ravenhead management team consciously used the Greengate experience as a template for its approach to this exercise. Given that it had to emulate, if not surpass, the cost structures of more modern competitor plants the task before Ravenhead was enormous:

we had to come from behind, 150 years behind to be precise, to match their cost structures.

The broad objectives of the Ravenhead restructuring programme were: to establish employment structures, systems and working practices aimed at increased cost effectiveness in human resource usage, based on a stronger sense of site and business identity; to facilitate team-based commitment to plant business objectives and the elimination of artificial divisions between employee groups; and to improve the quality of industrial relations by changing attitudes. The 'architecture' erected to support these changes comprised: new job definitions to enable optimum flexibility and mobility of employees; a single, integrated pay structure for all employees below middle management based on common job evaluation arrangements, participatively managed, and multi-union negotiations on pay and conditions; a simple grading structure with proper differentials and

relativities. The basis for attitudinal change was employee commitment
to a broad range of tasks, a commitment acknowledged by management in
the shape of an annual salary without additional ad hoc payments. All
employees – white and blue collar – were granted staff status and paid
according to a common, simplified pay structure. Computerised
attendance recording was introduced to facilitate flexible working
time arrangements. To facilitate these changes an average pay increase
of 12 per cent was agreed.

For management, a salaried pay structure offered the best prospects
of promoting attitudinal change amongst blue collar workers.
Pilkington's previous hourly paid structure had not only been highly
complicated by site bonuses but also incremental in nature. That is,
each additional or modified operative task resulted in further bonus
payments and yet another complication to an already over-complex
payment system. Harmonisation was the key to shifting manual workers
from an individualistic, task orientation to an attitude which
recognised that reward was based on the individual's contribution to
plant performance. The removal of overtime payments was equally
important in this respect. Overtime was seen as demotivating in that
poor attendance resulted in financial benefit for someone else. Paid
overtime also generated conflict between work groups with differing
possibilities for overtime. The payment and overtime system posed a
major barrier to the flexible use of labour. In a capital intensive
production process plant downtime was massively expensive. Moreover,
in a plant operating an exceedingly tight inventory system minor over-
runs in maintenance periods could have serious knock-on effects on
delivery times, particularly important in the context of ferocious
competition. The removal of overtime payments eliminated any implicit
incentive to ignore maintenance deadlines – with immediate payback in
maintenance scheduling and plant uptime. Crucially, harmonisation of
the payment system was not only regarded as important in its own right
but as an essential element of the framework for enabling ongoing
change.

The diffusion of the practices pioneered in Greengate to Ravenhead
threw the contrast between the traditional values of Pilkington's
labour and management into sharp relief. Before the market crisis of
the 1980s management had been highly bureaucratised in functional
hierarchies which engendered a remoteness from the market. Technical
excellence took precedence over commercial calculation, priorities
which could not be supported in the fight for survival. Product and
process developments were pursued for their own sake with little or no
conception of commercial viability; marketing was regarded as
supportive of invention and innovation rather than vice versa. The
change process was essential to reversing the priorities of Pilkington
managerial culture.

Managerial cultural change was implicit in the new principles of
work organisation: fewer jobs but bigger jobs with increased
responsibility and accountability; an emphasis on 'back to the line'
with fewer specialists; and fewer layers of accountability. In the
words of one senior personnel manager the intention was to ensure that
'a lot more people carried a lot more can'. During the long period of
growth management had gradually stripped production workers of

responsibility for product quality and process operations by creating an elaborate technical hierarchy: 'over the years when we encountered a problem we found an expert to deal with it'. This incurred penalties in both cost and motivational terms. By returning responsibility for quality and efficiency to individual workers Pilkington sought to improve routine problem-solving communications between plant management and the shopfloor without the distorting effect of technical intermediaries.

Flexibility was a key concept. It was conceptualised in three dimensions; first, tackling the obvious - the development of mechanical-electrical craftsmen, the elimination of craftsmen's assistants and a simplified job structure. Second, addressing the not so obvious - the elimination of quality inspectors, the development of maintenance supervision to run the process, and the development of a multi-functional office structure. The goal here was to push responsibility down to the lowest appropriate level. Third, enabling the future - laying the basis for the introduction of a multi-disciplined process craftsman, to gradually invest process workers with responsibility for routine maintenance and the elimination of craft supervision. 'Ultimately we want to eliminate craft supervision so that our craftsmen are essentially a self-supervising group'. How did Pilkington cross the Rubicon between imposing additional reponsibilities on employees and eliciting their active commitment to work reorganisation?

The choice of implementation method of these new working practices is now seen as crucial in gaining workforce acceptance. One alternative was for management to concoct 'an enormous package deal' in which work reorganisation was traded for bonuses. Such an approach was rejected as inimical to the broader purpose of the change agenda. A work reorganisation package devised solely by management and introduced via wage trade-offs could only secure workforce acceptance, it could not hope to win workforce commitment. Nor would negotiations conducted with full-time union officials expose shopfloor workers to the business necessities which underpinned the change process.

We wanted people to be open to the new structures. Perhaps most of all we wanted a process that was based on understanding business needs. If you say to somebody, 'Here's a package of changes and here's what you have to do and here's the extra money for them' you might well get them to do it but you don't get the understanding of why it's important. The understanding of why it was vital to us was the key for us if we wanted to continue ... and have it work and have it dynamic.

The goal was to establish a participative basis on which to build for the future. Ravenhead and Pilkington Group conducted multi-union discussions as the precursor to a more pervasive communication process. Central to this initiative was the dissemination of plant and divisional business plans geared to reinforcing local rather than corporate identities and loyalties.

The first port of call had nothing to do with work organisation. It was about the business plan. We spent several weeks going through our business situation and our route through to cost competitiveness in enormous detail, with product costs, margins, the breakdown of product costs, so that our people had a very, very fundamental understanding of where the business was now and an understanding of where we had to get to to enable us to be cost-competitive with our adversaries in the market. And we got outline agreement on a starting point and an objective.

The business plan was used as a point of departure, a vehicle for commitment and a reference point for all change initiatives. Any breakdown in negotiations returned to the business plan for reorientation, a clear identification of the inescapable fact of uncompetitiveness as the overwhelming problem to be solved:

> our trade unions saw the final implications of the business plan and thought, 'We can't agree to that', and all it needed was a reference back to the business plan and saying, 'Is there any doubt? Can it actually be solved in any other way? All this work we've done points to that fact'. We always got over the hurdle. So that starting point is important because it focusses on why and the needs rather than the difficulties.

Only after Pilkington had secured union agreement about the scale of the competitiveness problem did discussions about the actual organisation of work commence. Job structures were then analysed over a 5 month period which included extensive discussion with the whole workforce a process which, in retrospect, was vital to maximising employee commitment to the change process. Job structure planning reduced job profiles from 250 highly specified task clusters to 60 broad-based operative titles. Having agreed a new framework the next stage was job analysis and job evaluation to transform the abstract niceties of manpower planning into a viable division of labour. However, as one of the main players in this initiative explained, some of the major benefits of this process were unintended consequences rather than deliberately engineered.

> The analysis was absolutely key because, whilst we had new jobs they didn't exist in practice. They only existed in concept. So we had no job-holder we could go to and say, 'Let's write your job down in a framework that can be evaluated'. So we set up the job analysis multi-union teams, duos basically, one trade unionist, one manager. We sent them out armed with the information that this process had produced – the new job ideas – out into the factory to actually talk to job-holders and define the job. That was inspired. I can't claim that I understood when I set it up just how important it was. It's a sort of post hoc view this. But it was incredibly important because it meant that we had a multi-union, joint management-union team, which was going out and preaching the gospel. It was effectively selling this to the workforce and it was getting from the workforce a sense of realism too.

Between 7 and 8 per cent of the workforce were directly involved in the job analysis process while the purpose of change was reinforced by several week-long face-to-face briefings involving the whole workforce, further public testimony to the importance management ascribed to organisational change.

Payback was dramatic. Within twelve months of the process being set in motion in 1984 Pilkington Insulation Division recovered from annual losses of £3.5 million to £6.8 million profit. A positive basis for future gains had also been established with the integrated reward structure, multi-union negotiations. In short, the new structures provided 'enabling potential, a framework for ongoing change'. The participative nature of Pilkington's job analysis was vital in managing the change process because it ensured the practicality of work reorganisation while positive gains were made in terms of commitment by relying on employee representatives. For senior management an important lesson was the trade unions' capacity to absorb change and to become its agents.

The profound learning experience which occurred during the early 1980s has established a management style and a mutual receptivity to change which Pilkington believe will transform the company from a reactive to a proactive organisation capable of dealing with market uncertainty. As a result of the participative nature of the change process Pilkington believe. that 'we can continue to roll, albeit slowly, more slowly than the big bang which took place in 1985'. For labour there was a dual pay-off, job security – 'the carrot of getting to a point where everybody's job wasn't at risk' – and pay rises of 12 per cent made possible by enhanced productivity.

Work reorganisation was not the only way Pilkington responded to crisis in the insulation market. Internal organisational change was complemented by the acquisition of Cape Insulation, one of the company's major competitors who withdrew from the U.K. insulation unable 'to stand the pain of the price war'. This was not an entirely unexpected development since Pilkington deliberately accelerated the downward spiral of prices and profits as a defensive measure to protect market share and to test the resilience and commitment of new entrants to the marketplace. Pilkington share of the U.K. insulation market rose back to nearly 60 per cent, while sales volume returned to 1979 levels, albeit with an increased product range. The slimmed down Pilkington Insulation, reduced from around 2,500 to under 1200 employees, had achieved a cost structure forged during the price war while the Cape acquisition returned the company to its former market pre-eminence. While it is impossible to accurately proportion the contribution of the various factors in the division's recovery Pilkington themselves attribute 60 per cent of their recovery to organisational change and 40 per cent to strategic acquisition. This indicates, once again, the symbiotic relationship of market, strategy, structure, culture and working practices. Manufacturing excellence depends on complementary change along all these dimensions, not just on strategic realignment or structural adjustment.

CONCLUSION: THE PROCESS OF CHANGE

One momentous event in Pilkington's recent history has passed unmentioned: the unsuccessful £1.3 billion BTR bid for the company in

November 1986. Quite simply, this is because the BTR bid was incidental to the processes we have described. More significant was Pilkington's ability to ward off this challenge to its independence by pointing not only to favourable financial forecasts but also to the coherence of its business strategy. It is the organisational bases of Pilkington's renewed business strength which are of more enduring interest than the predatory motives of an industrial conglomerate.

Pilkington's senior management are conscious that the experience of a major business crisis was crucial in facilitating the acceptance of major change. However, the seminal importance of using the business plan as the spearhead of the change process was that knowledge of the depth of immediate crisis and the long-term uncertainties confronting Pilkington was diffused throughout the workforce rather than restricted to senior management. The participative nature of the change process both reinforced this corporate awareness of the centrality of business needs, of restoring productivity parity as the first step towards competitive advantage, as the prime imperative in corporate change. Indeed, 'business needs' has become the starting point, if not the lingua franca in internal company communications:

> The starting point is the business not the protection of jobs or whatever. The starting-point is the business — if that impinges on the job side we can see there's a problem there — whereas so often we start at the jobs end and say, 'We must start with this and to some extent let the business fit in'. So we've turned the thing on its head. That's the understanding we're trying to get ... business needs. That's the phrase that keeps coming all the way through the company, 'Business needs', 'Based on business needs', 'Manning based on business needs', 'Practices based on business needs', 'Structures based on business needs' ... That's the phrase going all the way through, driving through change.

On this basis, Pilkington's management are optimistic that the change programme deployed in response to the 'survival' crisis of the early 1980s established the structural, cultural and strategic bases for ongoing change. Strategically, the company has created a portfolio of established businesses, restored to competitiveness, and developing businesses based on reciprocally supporting emergent technologies in the electro-optical field. Culturally, Pilkington have made significant strides in modifying management and worker attitudes: on the one hand, a recognition that technical excellence alone is insufficient to guarantee commercial success; on the other hand, an increased awareness that job security and prosperity are dependent on business success, not vice versa. Such attitudes mean that Pilkington can take pre-emptive measures in preparation for any anticipated intensification of competitive pressures rather than be forced to wait until the company lurches towards competitive disaster.

The Pilkington change process has been distinctively British in its experiential, pragmatic, rather than programmatic, approach. Accordingly, the change process has itself been a learning experience for Pilkington's management. Pilkington are now assessing the change process with the intention of renewing the momentum of change, of accelerating evolutionary development. Key lessons derived from the early 1980s have been the immense benefits of the participative approach to change, particularly in terms of building employee understanding of, and commitment to, the change process. Indeed, management attribute greater importance to culture than reward in enabling change; reward is regarded as supportive of attitudinal change, rather than critical in its own right. This perception is supported by management's observation that the fastest progress in implementing change was made in those factories where there was the most involvement of the workforce in the change process.

Equally, management do not regard recent initiatives as an end in themselves, a particular response to a particularly pressing competitiveness problem. On the contrary, the main focus of management effort is how to accelerate change, not how to consolidate the changes which have already been made. Above all, Pilkington have conceptualised management as the prime mover of ongoing change. The philosophy and practices of participative management are being developed further with a newly developed cycle of strategy development involving more layers of management. Managerial flexibility is being encouraged by the development of multi-disciplinary management teams in product development and innovation exercises.

> Our latest initiatives are, essentially, trying to move our management teams faster into the future.

The changes dealt with in this chapter have not solved all of the company's problems. They constitute a partial solution and, perhaps more important, a platform for ongoing change. The major problem currently facing senior management is the role of the centre and central staff in the wake of decentralisation.

> The centre has been looked on historically as people who told you what you couldn't do, sort of policemen. 'Those bastards up there have stopped us.' I think they and we were trying to shift them to people who help and enable rather than stop.

In this they feel they have been reasonably successful. The centre monitor the performance of divisions and the solutions they devise to meet their problems and serve to disseminate successful ideas throughout the Group.

> There was some concern in the early days of decentralisation that the divisions were going to get very insular and protective of what they were doing and not want to share it. Fortunately we've been successful in stopping that. [For example] we bring the personnel directors together to share their plans and their views and to give colleagues an opportunity to learn from that. ... There might well be problems we notice and tell them to modify their plans accordingly.

Decentralisation, though, has been a guiding principle that has steadily grown in strength.

> The main board had known nothing other than hands on before that so it's taken them some time to learn how to avoid that. ... Like

decentralising pay bargaining. We were commercially decentralised in our minds but not giving the business managers the total wherewithal and freedom to actually get on with it.

The final logic of the decentralisation of decision-making is, perhaps, contained in the advice to 'think of Pilkington's as a holding company, bankers'.

Having decentralised and said to the divisions, 'Go off and run the business', the role of head office services is in urgent need of redefinition if the centre is to be seen as enabler rather than policeman. Consequently there have been changes in these service groups. In the central research and development laboratories the emphasis historically has been on process research, best exemplified in the development of the float glass process. Now it is equally focussed on product development and half of its annual budget is dedicated to divisional projects. The role of the other central service groups is more problematic and currently under review.

The changes that have been introduced also need monitoring in case they develop in unexpected directions, as has happened with flexitime, introduced as a way of using time more creatively for both the company's and the staff's benefit but now seen more as a convenience to workers than management. Here the pendulum of flexibility had swung too far.

Managers don't seem able to manage it for their benefit. That's one of the areas we're tightening up. It's also used as an excuse for accumulating hours off and we're stopping that. Managers still want the ability to flex and use people and ask them to come in at different times and stay on but they want to get rid of some of the weaknesses or you might call it abuses of the system.

Sub-contracting, too, might be a source of problems in the future. Its expanding usage has been 'all very emotive'. There have, for example, been 'battles in the computer area' due to the decision to contract out some management services work.

The key problem for the company will be how to maintain the momentum of the change process. The particular innovations necessary in the future might involve incremental adaptation of the forms already introduced or they might take a different shape. But whatever they are the willingness of the workforce, shopfloor and management alike, to participate in the search for creative solutions to the company's problems will be of crucial importance if those problems are to be continuously resolved. Here the role of management and management development to provide the Antony Pilkington's 'new breed' will be crucial.

The other thing that is interesting is how do you maintain the change process in a good time as opposed to a time of crisis. Can you? That comes back to superb management. The only people who make change are managers.

From this perspective the managerial process is the most important change arena.

4 Rank Xerox

INTRODUCTION

Rank Xerox Limited was established in Europe in 1956 as a joint venture between the Rank Organisation of England and the American enterprise, The Haloid Company, later Xerox Corporation, to exploit the revolutionary document copying process outside North America. The Rank Organisation is a minority shareholder within Rank Xerox, owning 49 per cent of the corporation's stock and drawing one third of corporate profits. However, despite this powerful minority holding, the Rank Organisation plays no significant strategic role in Rank Xerox's European or global management. Strategic management is Xerox's domain.

Rank Xerox is probably the largest joint venture in the world, employing nearly 30,000 people in its multi-national activities. In addition, Rank Xerox supports an estimated further 30,000 jobs through its supplier companies and the purchase of components and materials. The overwhelming bulk of the company's business − nearly 80 per cent − is located in Western Europe where it has five manufacturing plants − at Mitcheldean and Welwyn Garden City in the U.K.; at Venray in Holland; at Lille in France; and Coslada in Spain. While these plants provide important access to particular national markets they do not operate as stand-alone units but are integrated into the overall Xerox global value chain.

These factories serve both as finished machine plants and feeder plants and this complex activity has led the European manufacturing operation to be described as 'one plant in dispersion. (Rank Xerox 1985)

As we shall see, the inherent complexities of producing sophisticated technologies on a global basis were further complicated by rapid organisational change processes which blurred the boundaries between Rank Xerox and its supplier network.

Over the past three decades Xerox has become synonymous with document reproduction. Indeed, the company's core businesses remains the development, manufacture, marketing and maintenance of reprographic products such as xerographic copiers and duplicators, with obvious related interests in office supplies. It is precisely this legacy which is both Rank Xerox's greatest marketing strength and weakness. On the one hand, the company's historic customer base is a key competitive advantage in an increasingly saturated market while, on the other hand, the strength of consumer identification is with Rank Xerox's past products, not the integrated business systems which the company regard as its future. For over a decade Xerox has attempted to break out of its reprographic fastness, an area with limited growth potential but a seemingly unlimited capacity to attract ferocious competition. This chapter will examine the organisational implications of Rank Xerox's strategic decision to link long-term corporate survival to this seismic shift from producing reprographic machinery to marketing 'the Office of the Future'.

MARKET PRESSURES AND CORPORATE RESPONSES

From its foundation in 1956 to the mid-1970s Rank Xerox dominated its core markets, a dominance underpinned by the company's technological lead in product and processes. During this twenty year period Xerox worldwide experienced constant growth. Even the entry of new copier manufacturers in the early 1970s did not damage the company's quasi-monopoly profits which grew approximately 20-30 per cent per year. By 1983 the impact of Japanese competition, notably Canon and Ricoh, had almost halved profit levels from their 1977 peak of £300 million. Confronted by aggressive price-cutting competitors Rank Xerox initially responded by seeking to preserve market share, at the expense of profit margins. However, the failure of this defensive strategy is evident from the fact that during the same period market share dropped from 90 per cent to 45 per cent of the copier market, including the decimation of Rank Xerox's share of the fast-growing, low-volume end of the range. Even in the more profitable mid-volume and high-volume end of the market the company now has the status of major player rather than monopolist. Just as we saw in Ford, Rank Xerox primarily understood the Japanese challenge in terms of a price war, a trade battle rather than a confrontation in which business organisation was itself a key factor in competitive advantage. However, unlike Ford, the organisational learning process was accelerated by direct access to Japanese best practice through another of the Xerox joint ventures - Fuji Xerox.

Organisational learning has been, and will continue to be, crucial to Rank Xerox's change strategy. For Rank Xerox Chairman Derek Hornby, the major theme of the company's development in the 1980s has been 'innovation into profit' and the major question to be answered, 'can we teach ourselves to change?' (Hornby 1986). If the necessity of change was the compelling force of ferocious market pressures then the direction of change was equally clear-cut; Rank Xerox had to understand and emulate Japanese competition while extending its product base into higher value added aspects of office automation. Nor could Rank Xerox regard corporate change as a short-term, piecemeal process of organisational and strategic realignment, a temporary expedient to meet abnormal conditions during the recession. In its historic core markets Rank Xerox could anticipate with some certainty intensifying competition in a reprographic market rapidly becoming saturated. Similarly, moving into the parallel office automation markets offered no permanent refuge for the company. The technological promise of convergent technologies in the business systems sector will ensure that the already indistinct boundaries within and between hardware and software markets will disappear, with a ratchet effect on competition as manufacturers are increasingly drawn to a common marketplace. These two factors, the salience of the Japanese challenge and the anticipated permanence of unstable competitve conditions, have been critical in shaping the contours of Rank Xerox's change strategy. The distinctive features of the Rank Xerox change process are: change is conceptualised and operationalised as a permanent rather than temporary feature of Rank Xerox's development; change is pervasive and rapid rather than piecemeal and slow; change is radical and thoroughgoing rather than experimental and marginal; change is programme-driven rather than experiential; organisational change is central to, rather than derivative of, competitive strategy. In the market context confronting Rank Xerox only profound technological, production, marketing and organisational innovation could ensure corporate survival.

The need for change has been met in a range of areas. A major decision was taken to simplify and restructure the business, to change company culture and to transform working practices. Major changes were introduced in the management of the organisation, primary examples of which are decentralisation with devolution of authority, a substantial reduction in manpower, competitive benchmarking, employee involvement, Just in Time management, and networking. There has also been a marked cultural change away from the indifferent 'arrogance' of the virtual monopolist to a customer-centred approach. The company reassessed its business strategy and its location in the information technology market. Most importantly, there was a fundamental change in the company's marketing philosophy — a move away from the maximisation of sales of standard products to niche marketing based on in-depth analyses of customer needs and the concept of total office design. Long-term business strategy now focusses on the Office of the Future, the first phase of which is document management — the integrated processing, creating, storing, printing and distributing of business documents — traditional areas of Rank Xerox expertise. It is precisely this expertise, and Rank Xerox's extensive customer base, which will form the bridgehead into the wider office systems market. Current change initiatives have, therefore, a double function; to ensure short-term competitiveness in existing reprographic markets and to enable the transition into the office automation market in the medium-term.

If environmental pressures were the prime stimuli for organisational change then the precise pattern of the change process was decisively shaped by the experience of another Xerox joint venture company, Fuji Xerox of Japan. Fuji Xerox, founded in 1962 by a liaison with Fuji Photo Film, had experienced a similar development trajectory to Rank Xerox thirteen years of explosive growth in revenues, profits and personnel followed by a flatter demand growth and intensified competition during the mid-1970s. In the context of the smaller volume and more highly segmented Far Eastern copier markets competitive advantage hinged upon increasing customer sensitivity and decreasing the costs of model change (Porter 1986, p.51). In short, in manufacturing the critical balance lay between the efficient exploitation of economies of scale on the one hand, and frequent product change across a shifting range of models on the other. Fuji Xerox's ability to respond to the emergence of new competitors such as Ricoh and Canon was further hampered by inadequate product development (Jacobson and Hillkirk 1986). For Fuji Xerox business turnaround began in 1976 with the New Xerox Movement, a total quality control process centred on statistical quality control, teamwork and participative management. A new business philosophy was developed based on dedication to continuous quality improvement using statistical quality control techniques pioneered by W. Edward Deming and Joseph M. Juran.

Key principles adopted from Deming included:

Top management must make the pursuit of quality a corporate goal. Inspections of products after they have been manufactured is wasteful.
The emphasis should be placed on preventing errors, not detecting them after they occur.
The use of statistical control methods, if rigorously and continuously applied, can help to produce quality products. (Xerox Corporation 1986, p.4)

The company accepted Juran's definition of quality as 'fitness for use' and his notion that the basic quality mission of a company is 'to make products which meet the needs of the user' because 'fitness for use is properly determined from the viewpoint of the user, not the manufacturer'. Impressed by Juran's 1966 prediction that the Japanese were headed for world quality leadership they also accepted his view that

The pursuit of quality is a never-ending process. ...Massive training is a prerequisite of quality. The entire management of a company must be trained in how to attain, control and improve quality. Quality requires hands-on leadership by senior management including the chief executive officer. Without that attention and leadership, quality efforts are meaningless. (Xerox Corporation 1986, p.5)

Juran's all-embracing quality message had a deep resonance with established Japanese management practices. The Japanese life-time

employment system for core employees leaves no latitude to hire and
fire employees, so the management and training of personnel is a
matter of strategic importance. Employees are recruited not to
specific jobs but to Fuji Xerox. Job rotation, ideally every four or
five years, occurs within both technical and non-technical areas and
produces managers who recognise no artificial demarcation line between
business and technical decision-making. Equally significant is the
role life-time job security plays in promoting harmonious
relationships between management and workforce. As one Fuji Xerox
employee explained, this allows collective bargaining to be conducted
within a framework dictated by business performance:

> The trade union is outspoken in negotiating for wages and benefits
> but never takes any action that will weaken the company. There are
> no strikes - if there were, what would happen to the customer? We
> all understand the concept of co-destiny. (Giles and Starkey 1987,
> p.20)

The phenomenal turnaround achieved by Fuji Xerox - annual revenue
growth of 25 per cent and profits by 28 per cent by 1982 - and the
deteriorating position of Xerox worldwide reinforced the power of the
Japanese exemplar. The key link between Fuji Xerox and the rest of the
corporation was the role played by David Kearns, Xerox's Chairman.
Kearns drew two lessons from visits to Japan - the paramount
importance of product quality and of employee commitment. As a result,
he determined to change the culture of Xerox in the way that Fuji
Xerox had done (Giles and Starkey 1987, p.20).

There is apparently something of a paradox here. The example of Fuji
Xerox had offered Xerox a unique window onto Japanese management
practices over a long period. And yet this unique learning resource
remained largely untapped until the late 1970s. The reasons for
Xerox's corporate indifference are not difficult to find. For one
thing the corporation's huge monopoly profits during a boom lasting
three decades permitted it to cover grotesque operating
inefficiencies. Nor were Japanese practices, which Xerox understood as
being culture specific, easily diffused throughout the corporation. At
the very least, the emulation of Japanese techniques would require a
complete revolution in corporate management. It was the coincidence of
events - the corporation's financial and marketing crisis - and
exemplar, in the shape of Fuji Xerox, which provided the unique set of
circumstances in which Xerox and Rank Xerox began the massive change
process regarded as essential to corporate survival.

The first step in the change process was to identify just how far
Rank Xerox and Xerox had fallen behind its new competitors in terms of
productivity, quality and design. Xerox President David Kearns was the
critical catalyst in triggering an emulative benchmarking exercise
based not on Rank Xerox's historic performance in these areas but on
'best practice' across industry, including international comparisons.
For Kearns, a key mistake of the 1970s was the company's failure to
understand the organisational bases of Japanese business or the cost
structure of Japanese manufacturing (McLellan 1984). Rank Xerox's
benchmarking exercise involved identifying competitive gaps in

engineering costs, product quality, product lead times, inventory levels and, most innovatively, in routine business administration.

It was during this process that the Fuji Xerox experience assumed a more tangible role in corporate change. Until the benchmarking exercise had begun Fuji Xerox had no more than a symbolic status within the corporation; a powerful, yet distant, image of what could be achieved but with little practical importance for Western management practices. Comparisons between equivalent Fuji Xerox and Rank Xerox plants producing similar machines revealed the true extent of Japanese competitive advantage; Western manufacturing costs were roughly double those of the Far East. Given the corporation's strategic decision to use reprographics as the financial and marketing launching pad into the business systems market, Rank Xerox had two broad alternatives when faced with such damning cost comparisons. Xerox could deploy these statistics as a stick to beat the backs of Western management, a threat used to intensify existing patterns of work organisation. For Kearns, such a negative use of benchmarking would have merely confirmed the very Western management practices which underlay the corporation's ever-growing competitive disadvantage. Moreover, such an implicitly coercive approach would fail to address the second dimension Kearns identified as essential to Fuji Xerox success — employee commitment to company goals and to the change process. Alternatively, benchmarking could be used more positively, as a stimulus for organisational change which would allow Xerox to compete on equal organisational terms with Far Eastern companies. Xerox chose the latter course.

LEADERSHIP THROUGH QUALITY

Competitive benchmarking across the Xerox organisation was the prelude to 'one of the company's most innovative decisions' (Hornby 1986): the decision to initiate a massive training programme as the vehicle for a profound company-wide change process. Before 1979 90 per cent of Rank Xerox business had been in copier rental. Capital realised by the sale of these machines was reinvested in training. If the scale of this investment demonstrated the seriousness of Rank Xerox's intent then the source of the finance confirmed the company's new marketing strategy and the centrality of organisational change to this new business direction.

Rationalisation in the early 1980s improved Rank Xerox's competitiveness but the company's strategic planners warned that further changes were imperative if the company was to compete in the long term with firms like IBM and AT&T in the reprographics and office systems markets. The task confronting Xerox's strategic management was not simply diffusing some of the operating principles used by Fuji Xerox but to establish the organisational and cultural bases for maintaining change as a permanent feature of corporate life. The Leadership Through Quality strategy was developed during 1983 by a senior management team drawn from all the major units of Xerox. As with competitive benchmarking, David Kearns played a key role in the formation of the strategy which emphasises quality as the vehicle of, and focus for, change.

70

Leadership through Quality is a long-term, company-wide, ongoing process aimed at transforming processes of decision-making, processes of interaction among employees and the way the company relates to its customers. Its goals are summarised in the 1985 International Report:

Xerox is a quality company. Quality is the basic principle for Xerox. Quality means providing our external and internal customers with innovative products and services that fully satisfy their requirements. Quality improvement is the job of every Xerox employee.

The strategic goals of Leadership through Quality, then, are quality, product reliability and cost. Quality is defined in terms of satisfying customer requirements – 'conformance to customer requirements' (Xerox Corporation 1986, p.7) – and the achievement of quality is based on the prevention of errors rather than their rectification. Quality is also measured in terms of costs incurred when customer requirements are not satisfied – costs of non-conformance to customer requirements such as design changes, rework, scrap, service recalls, unnecessary administration. The costs of quality – the costs of conformance – include training, quality workshops, discovering customer requirements, quality inspection and audit.

Whereas the conventional performance standard for quality is some acceptable level of defects or errors, the quality performance standard in Xerox is 'products and services that fully satisfy the requirements of our customers'. Whereas the conventional system of achieving quality is to detect and correct products after they have been completed, Xerox emphasizes the 'prevention of errors'. Whereas the conventional system for measurement of quality relies on indices, Xerox measures quality by the 'costs we incur when we do not satisfy customer requirements'. (Xerox Corporation 1986, pp.7-8)

The principle of quality costing applies not only to Rank Xerox's external customers but also to each workgroup's internal customers within the Rank Xerox value chain. Importantly, quality costing is a collaborative rather than a competitive process in which the participants in the transaction share a common analytical framework, exchange information and recognise their mutual inter-dependence within the overall company strategy.

According to Ronald Magnin, Managing Director of Rank Xerox, Leadership through Quality represents 'the most significant and exciting challenge we have had as an organization'. This view is endorsed by David Mercer, Director of Quality: 'Leadership through Quality is a strategy of change which may very well be the most significant that Xerox has ever embarked upon ... In a very real sense, it will fundamentally change the Corporation's approach to doing business' (International Report 1986). Quality means 'conforming to customer requirements, in other words, giving the customer what he wants, not what we think he ought to have'. Leadership through Quality is a 'strategy of change ... undertaken for very fundamental business reasons':

The principles of focussing on the customer and developing a supportive management style using the Quality tools and processes will enable the company to meet the objectives set, namely return on assets, customer satisfaction and market share.

This new quality orientation marks a significant shift in emphasis in management priorities. Previously, financial measures were the sole criterion of business effectiveness, now satisfying external customer requirements is regarded as the essential complement to financial success, in prospect is Xerox's move adoption of customer satisfaction as its premier business priority. Such a change of business priorities would entail overthrowing the Western preoccupation with the short-term goal of return on investment with the long-term Japanese perspective based on optimising the organisation's position in the market.

Five mechanisms for change form the basis of Leadership through Quality: standards and measurement; reward and recognition; training; communications; and the use of senior management as role models for the process. A central goal in Leadership through Quality training has been the development and dissemination of a common language to articulate company goals and a shared approach to routine problem-solving and personal interactions within the company. The basis of this 'company language' is a range of inter-personal skills based on successful interactions between salesmen and customers. Throughout Rank Xerox each problem is analysed in the same way, with possible solutions evaluated and prioritised in terms of the relative costs of conformance and non-conformance.

Xerox's enormous investment in training has been crucial to ensuring maximum employee 'literacy' in the new company language. Reflecting the Fuji Xerox maxim that the only way to win employee support is to demonstrate managerial commitment to change, training has 'cascaded' down through the company – starting with David Kearns and corporate headquaters in Connecticut! Defined in terms of man-years, training is now the equivalent of the sixth largest operating company within the Xerox corporation. At each level management train their subordinates in Leadership through Quality techniques and agree quality criteria for their operations; each layer of management therefore participates in Leadership through Quality training – which takes four or five days – at least three times. The intention is not only to guarantee managerial familiarity with Leadership through Quality principles but to publicly identify each manager with Leadership through Quality. The 'cascade' approach ensures managers are role models in a continuing learning process, in preference to training by anonymous 'outsiders' whose contact with each workgroup is necessarily limited. Similarly, workgroup teams or 'family groups' are established to carry the process forward on an ongoing basis so that training is not just a 'one-off' event. Each unit now has a Director of Quality responsible for training in the new analytical skills and to develop improved communication processes, increase employee involvement and modify ways of recognising and rewarding employees.

The change process has impacted on all levels of the organisation. For management, it has involved a shift from a competitive, political managerial ethos to an open management style based on a structured, participative approach to problem-solving and decision-making. The use of Leadership through Quality analytical techniques necessitates the articulation of clear and consistent objectives which in turn allows problems to be brought out into the open, clarified by group analysis and, hopefully, resolved.

> One of the big things about Leadership through Quality is the cultural change we're promoting. We're moving from being a fiercely competitive, confrontational style of management – where managers fought managers – very political, very competitive – towards a more open style of management where people can actually say what they like without it dropping them in the s--t.

More open communication means that employees are kept informed of organisational objectives and priorities and of their own performance so that Leadership through Quality is always explicitly linked to corporate strategic goals. However, as one senior manager revealed, the very goals of the Leadership through Quality process may engender managerial resistance, particularly given the company's inherited managerial culture.

> Quality is about power-sharing, about giving power to the customer and to subordinates. If you allow people to influence you, you give up expert power. But people build up their reputation with expert power. To give up goes against the organisation's power culture. Xerox encourages stars and highfliers, not self-effacing managers like Japan. (Giles and Starkey 1987, p.43)

The inevitable clashes between the heritage of the past and Rank Xerox's vision of a new organisational shape for the future. A particular problem for Rank Xerox is how to ground the quality precepts into the company's formal and informal reward systems. As one manager explained:

> If an individual is achieving results in the eyes of his supervisor, no-one is really bothered whether the results have been achieved in a quality way. People are still judged and promoted on content, not on process. (Giles and Starkey 1987, p.42)

In other words, there is a perceptible divergence between Rank Xerox's new processual philosophy and recognition and reward within the company, a divergence which reflects an older and still pervasive value system. This deeply embedded individual achievement orientation is being challenged by conscious moves by Rank Xerox to reward the use of Leadership through Quality techniques. Sales staff, for example, are no longer simply paid commission on monthly sales figures but are rewarded for generating longer-term revenues (Foster 1987). By linking incentives to long-term revenue growth rather than short-term turnover Rank Xerox not only reward 'quality thinking' but also ensure that grassroots sales activity furthers the company's overriding strategic goal – to gain, or regain, market share.

Structural change in Rank Xerox has involved two main elements. First, International Headquarters, which coordinates Xerox's worldwide network, was reorganised into a Strategic Business Unit structure based on different market segments. Xerox's corporate headquarters deliberately adopted an enabling, rather than a directive, role in the change process which entailed the rapid devolution of authority to the operational level, now directly accountable for business results. This leaner structure both lowered corporate overhead costs, clarified managerial accountability and accelerated the decision-making process.

The second structural change reflects the total process perspective implemented by the corporation: structural, strategic and cultural change are regarded as inter-dependent dimensions of organisational change. Purchased materials represent some 80 per cent of Rank Xerox's product cost — forty times direct labour costs — a fact which forced Rank Xerox to include their supplier network in the change process. For this reason, changing relationships with the supplier network has paralleled work reorganisation within Rank Xerox. A central part of this process has been the Materials and Logistics programme based on the use of Just In Time (JIT) principles of management. This is an overall materials management strategy focussing on product and material cost and quality. Suppliers' cooperation, therefore, was essential to closing the competitive gap identified by the benchmarking process. The materials management strategy, therefore, aims at improving the quality of suppliers' contributions to Rank Xerox as well as improving the assembly of final products and strategy encompasses the following elements: the consolidation of the supplier base, reducing it from 5000 to 300; contracts for worldwide volume; single sourcing; a long-term cooperative business relationship with suppliers; supplier participation as an integral part of product design and development; full sharing of parts, functional and assembly requirements and cost and quality targets; cost reduction by benchmarking and operations improvement, not by elimination of profit margins; Just In Time manufacturing.

Just In Time management (JIT) has generally been limited to experiments within single plants in Western companies, a pattern which neglects the equally important role of supplier companies in the Japanese model. In Rank Xerox, by contrast, JIT has been central to work reorganisation in company plants and the synchronisation of production throughout the supplier network. How, then, has Rank Xerox conceptualised JIT? For Rank Xerox, JIT aims at uniform plant load, reduction of inventory and rapid response to changes in customer requirements. It is based on the establishment of accurate manufacturing cycle times so that the entire production system can eventually be synchronised with the sales rate. This depends on process flow redesign, the redesign of the production process using small workgroups to ensure faster throughput, to reduce space requirements and to minimise material handling. By reducing production set-up times and facilitating smooth changeovers the organisation is able to move towards small production lot sizes and to improve productivity and flexibility.

Of crucial importance in the JIT process is a quality improvement programme in which quality is explicitly defined, quality variances analysed and quality problems identified, and 'making it right first time' is emphasised. The ultimate aim is 'zero defects'. JIT fosters pull system scheduling so that the manufacture of components is only authorised when they are required, thus reducing unnecessary inventory. It simplifies control of work-in progress and makes the production system more sensitive to fluctuations in demand by establishing clear stock upper limits and developing clear signals for stock delivery. In Japan the need for new stock is signalled by kanban, coloured tokens that signify existing stock has reached a specified low level. An integral feature is installing this control system throughout the supplier network. By integrating the supplier into the quality assurance process JIT emphasises the cooperative relationship between supplier and company. Parts quality and delivery certification by suppliers are a prerequisite. The company insists that suppliers operate on JIT principles and embrace statistical process control as a guarantee of the quality of their products and as part of the Xerox certification process. This enables the following material logistics: just-in-time deliveries, frequent deliveries of small batches, direct shipment to other manufacturing sites and distribution centres.

By involving its suppliers in product design and development and in the implementation of JIT management Rank Xerox is progressively transforming its relationships with suppliers from low-trust spot bargaining to high-trust inter-dependence based on single sourcing. Such a transformation will effectively blur the boundaries between Rank Xerox and the supplier network which produces vital semi-manufactured components. The impact of this major modification to the organisation's external boundaries has been compounded by internal realignment, specifically the withdrawal of the guaranteed privileged status previously accorded Rank Xerox's own manufacturing plants. The introduction of JIT management throughout Rank Xerox and its supplier network has not only had a significant impact on company competitiveness but has also accelerated the process of cultural change by exposing individual Rank Xerox plants and workgroups to real and immediate market pressures within the company's value chain. In essence, internal relations previously based on hierarchies and bureaucratic authority are being gradually transformed into actual or surrogate market transactions. Inside Rank Xerox the disintegrative potential of these profound structural changes are being counteracted by cultural realignment emphasising participation and commitment to common goals.

Managing the complex materials flows within and between Rank Xerox and its supplier network has been centralised at the European Logistics Centre, Venray, Holland. In addition, the Venray plant where JIT was implemented in 1983 provides the benchmark for the rest of the Rank Xerox. Along with the optimisation of parts supply, the company has also rationalised space allocation. At Welwyn, for example, computerised carousel units have reduced the size of the stores area by 60 per cent and improved control and forward planning of component flows within the factory. For the Welwyn manufacturing manager, the combined effect of computerised forward planning, JIT and the quality philosophy makes cooperative relations between Rank Xerox and the supplier network a mutual business imperative:

> We talk to our suppliers about quality and about the principles of just in time deliveries. By working with them to the extent that we even let them know what our long term order book looks like, we aim to eliminate reject materials ending up on the shopfloor. (cited Grikitis, 1985)

The ultimate aim of JIT throughout Xerox is to have one month's worth of stock, or 'twelve inventory turns' per year. The company buys in a world-wide marketplace so that materials are sourced globally with major suppliers located in North America, Europe and the Far East. A large proportion of component contracting is also undertaken on a world-wide basis, thus allowing the company to take advantage of volume pricing with multi-national suppliers, ensuring competitive material costs. Much effort is put into ensuring that suppliers' products comply with the best engineering component specification and standard through quality assurance teams linked to particular suppliers. The company also 'certifies' its suppliers.

> With a vendor base across the world, supplying more than 5000 different parts, the company has set a target of 90 per cent for the number of certified parts it uses, that is which do not need inspecting as goods inward. At present, this figure stands a 73.4 per cent, with a reject rate of 200ppm for parts coming out of the stores. (Grikitis 1985)

The impact of these changes in continental and British plants has been dramatic. Since 1980 assembly costs have been halved, inventory levels reduced by 65 per cent, quality improved by 89 per cent and transport costs down 40 per cent. Yet despite these formidable gains the Venray management does not yet consider its performance good enough to survive, in the long term, against Far-East competition.

On the shopfloor, the strategic choice to abandon standardised mass production for mid-volume specialisation has forced work organisation and cultural change to the top of the managerial agenda. The successful manufacture of products of widely differing size, complexity and quantity within short time-scales is dependent upon the joint effects of more sophisticated technology, especially testing equipment, and employee commitment. Production workgroups are responsible for their own quality control, reduced production faults results in declining rectification time and higher output.

The Welwyn Garden City plant produces micro chip control boards in over 150 different configurations and a variety of high-voltage power supply units. In a typical month as many as 60 to 70 different types of board are produced of 'widely varying complexity and run sizes'. Management attribute the survival of the plant to the workforce's commitment to the Leadership through Quality process, particularly the daily Quality Assurance audit routine; for example:

> a nine person team on the shop floor has taken electronic test (a key quality and cost driver) from eight per cent below to five

percent above plan levels. Thus the boards achieve 93-94 per cent first time pass rates (an excellent standard for the industry) freeing up to 50 people to build more boards, as opposed to diagnosing or reworking test failures. (International Report 1986).

Leadership through Quality techniques have also permitted production staff access to the design process as quasi-consumers, an influential as opposed to peripheral input to product design. Indeed, such has been the success of the Welwyn plant in this respect that it is being used as the testing ground for collapsing the distinctions between design, production and service engineering; again, a reflection of the Japanese model. Computer Integrated Manufacturing (CIM) is vital to maintaining Rank Xerox's lead in producing the integrated circuit boards which allow the development of ever smaller and inexpensive copiers. In CIM a database of information about a product generated during Computer Aided Design (CAD) is used to drive machine tools and robots and monitor material quantities in conjunction with sales ordering computers. Eventually it is predicted that CIM will lead to the breaking down of the traditional demarcations between design, manufacturing and service engineers, thus preparing the way for the 'multi-functional', flexible engineer. The immediate objective is higher quality product at lower cost and reducing the time lag between product design and manufacture to increase organisational responsiveness to changing consumer demand. Here again we see the distinctive strength of Rank Xerox's total process approach which meshes short-term marketing tactics with longer-term organisational goals.

What motivates the workforce to involve itself so integrally in these developments? For one thing, the impact of competitive pressures on shopfloor attitudes through structural change in the Xerox value chain and the constant dissemination of business information serves as a reminder of the need to maintain the momentum of progress. More positively, motivation has also been stimulated by changing the quality of the working environment, emphasising teamwork and a supportive working climate. A key element here is the stress laid on the 'power of recognition'. A supportive climate is defined as one in which positive behaviour, positive in the sense of promoting quality, is linked to recognition and reward. Internal attitude surveys revealed that Rank Xerox employees did not feel adequately rewarded for their contributions to the company. Subsequent surveys – and the massive leaps in labour productivity and quality – demonstrated the tangible effects of the training programme and the extension of Leadership through Quality processes. Therefore, quality inspection is now linked to recognition and reward when quality is achieved and recognition and reward are seen as important means of maintaining motivation.

NETWORKING: A NEW WAY OF ORGANISING MANAGERIAL WORK

Networking is the most well-known of Rank Xerox's innovations in work organisation, mainly on account of the intense media interest it has aroused and the idea that it provides the model for the future of managerial work. Networking is only one of a series of company experiments with new patterns of work and has to be seen in the context of the changes previously analysed. Networking is

> an experimental system of work whereby selected and trained volunteers leave the parent company, and establish their own limited company, which in turn contracts to provide services to the parent company among other customers, using a microcomputer link as a D.P. [data processing] and communications tool. (Judkins, n.d.)

It is not, according to the company, a means of moving people from the core workforce to peripheral status. Networkers are predominantly drawn from managerial, professional and executive levels of the company and the networking relationship has developed because the company does not want to lose them. It is not unlikely that they will return to the company on a full-time basis in due time after having been provided with the opportunity to try out their entrepreneurial skills, which was their main motive in leaving.

Networking, therefore, was, in part, the company's response to their professional workers' needs although it did offer the organisation considerable benefits.

> Networking has a threefold origin. First, competitive pressure on our organisation intensified, with price-cutting beginning to appear as a regular feature of the office equipment business. The profit erosion to which this led threatened the high level of major Research and Development expenditure required to ensure a consistent supply of high quality future products. Overhead costs naturally came under scrutiny. Second, we had observed, over a period of years, the tendency for creative people to be relatively mobile around organisations, seeking the ability to regulate their own work, rather than being controlled in detail. As our organisation depends on many such creative people, it was appropriate to research ways of retaining their skills without stifling their creativity. Third, the technology - the microcomputer capable of transmitting data over telephone lines - was at last becoming widely available at a low cost. (Judkins, West and Drew 1985, p.17)

In terms of the total cost of employment the networking relationship offered the company substantial opportunities in the cutting of overheads, such as facilities costs (rent, rates, depreciation, maintenance, energy costs, security, etc.) which are inflationary, out of the company's control, sterile (adding nothing to the value of the company's products), and do not motivate people in any real sense (Judkins, West and Drew 1985, pp.18-19). The total cost to the company in terms of facilities, oncosts and salary of an employee earning £10,000 salary is actually £27,000!

Networking, then, is

> a new method of organising work which allows substantial real cuts in sterile overhead costs, builds on the prospects opened by new

78

office technology and seeks to enhance motivation, achievement, and self-regulation opportunities. (Judkins, West and Drew 1985, p.114)

Only a small percentage (5 per cent) of central staff are involved, not many more than 50 people and it is applicable only to information workers and not process or manufacturing work. The relationship with the company is structured to enhance independence and to reduce isolation. Only a maximum of 50 per cent of the work of the networker is with Xerox. Networkers become part of an extended 'Xerox family', spending one day a fortnight on average in the organisation and able to join Xanadu (the Xerox Association of Networkers and Distributed Utilities), a support association made up of suppliers of services to Xerox which facilitates the exchange of business information and provides group purchasing and services. Advantages to the company, besides the saving on overheads, include the definition of contracts in output terms, so that a fee is paid for the finished job and not for time worked. As a result output and quality of output is clearly defined, the first time this has been possible in many staff areas, and a mutually acceptable mechanism for the control of professional work is inaugurated. Contracts are negotiated as with any other Xerox supplier. Networkers gain in this in that they calculate that they take only half the time to complete the same amount of work when they are self-employed. The company also benefits because networkers bring to the company

their deeper knowledge of the company which makes the networker's project work more relevant than that of an outside consultant. (Judkins, West and Drew 1985, p.49)

Networking has led to a reanalysis of work structures within the organisation by initiating a whole set of new needs in organisation development focussing on what core staff development is necessary to manage the loose federation of work of which networking is a part. A new kind of managerial vision is necessary.

The return to smaller semi-independent work units is one which will require a greater emphasis on such managerial skills as planning, setting quality standards and negotiation. The manager in this structure will be operating as the purchaser of services from a number of companies, and both managers and suppliers will require a clear vision of the strategies and outputs needed. (Judkins, West and Drew 1985, p.114)

Here the Quality process was important in aiding managers in the establishment of acceptable quality standards and in the design and scheduling of work. This was considered necessary because 'we had, in fact, successfully trained the networkers how to sell, but none of our managers how to buy, with quite predictable results!' (Judkins, West and Drew 1985, p.98). Networking also impacted on the work of support staff. Initially occupying a gatekeeper role for networkers they are increasingly taking on executive functions with the growth of computer power and the importance of their IT skills. 'Decision support executives' is the term by which they are described with a host of

staff development programmes currently being developed to help them in
their evolving and critical role.

The main problems arising out of the networking innovation, then,
have been the definition of output and quality standards and the
training and development of core staff, particularly managers and
support staff. As the organisation seeks to adapt to the changing work
patterns it has itself created with its new organisational structures
and its technology developments, an intrinsic part of this process,
like the implementation of successful just in time systems, is the
analysis and, perhaps for the first time, the real understanding of
the kind of business they are in.

CONCLUSION

Change in Rank Xerox was prompted by the slow growth of the copier
market in the late 1970s and an anticipation of the emerging
dematurity of the office technology market in the 1980s. From the
first, Rank Xerox recognised that profound organisational change was
essential to regaining and maintaining competitive edge rather than
incidental to strategic choice. The experience of Fuji Xerox in
similar market conditions was crucial to Rank Xerox's
conceptualisation of the multi-dimensional and multi-temporal nature
of successful organisational change. Accordingly, the Leadership
through Quality programme was conceived of as a series of structural
realignments and common processual techniques which is embedding a
culture of change as an everyday and ongoing process rather than as a
vehicle for a period of specific, limited reorganisations. The change
process has blurred the boundaries of the firm. In this respect,
interest in the celebrated networkers has overshadowed the more
important alterations to the relationships between Rank Xerox and its
supplier network. This has had a reciprocal impact on Rank Xerox's
internal functioning; reducing what were previously sharp breaks in
the Rank Xerox value chain has consolidated the identification of
succeeding workgroups as 'customers' with a degree of choice within
the extended Rank Xerox production network. The deliberate creation of
structures and processes specifically geared towards organisational
realignment makes change within Rank Xerox a self-perpetuating
process, centrally stimulated but dependent for its momentum on
grassroots commitment to the Leadership through Quality techniques.

The overall aim of the changes introduced in the 1980s has been to
regain leadership of its markets through the emphasis on quality. A
key problem has been organising to maintain momentum so that
particular change initiatives are seen as not just one-off projects
but as 'something we have to do everyday and forever'. Cultural change
is regarded as essential to regaining current competitiveness and,
equally important, establishing the long-term attitudinal and
processual bases for successful survival in the wider office systems
market. Change, in other words, and a culture not only receptive to,
but stimulative of, organisational innovation must become self-
perpetuating. Here the role of top managers as role models to sustain
the process is seen as of paramount importance in the effort to
cascade the principles down through the organisation. In employee

relations the principal aim is to remove traditional barriers between employees and managers by generating a common viewpoint concerning corporate strategy. The change effort overall makes the job of management 'enormously demanding':

It's the old one about trying to drain the swamp while you're surrounded by alligators. It's a vicious circle but you've got to break out. Otherwise you're just fire-fighting forever.

There is a poignant undercurrent to this organisational anecdote; a sense of future purpose counterpointed by an appreciation of current business need. Nor does this simply reflect the frustrations of an individual manager but the recurring clash between organisational visions and current exigencies. However, even where the tension between innovation and efficiency is currently resolved in favour of the latter Rank Xerox personnel retain a distinctive world-view about future possibilities. The central personnel department — responsible for the networker initiative — has been forced back to a more reactive mode as a result of rationalisation thus compromising long-term strategic personnel planning. But this is construed by some as an oppportunity for more profound organisational innovation:

It is often the ones who lag behind who leapfrog ahead. Staff reductions might give Xerox the impetus to look to technology for help with its human resource management. (Giles and Starkey 1987, p.47)

One wonders, though, what the implications are for employees if the search for future success is predicated primarily on technological innovation. One perspective on networking is that it demonstrates significant potential for reducing the overheads associated with the employment of core staff. Advances in desktop publishing raise the same issue. Commenting on the chimera of the 'paperless office' one industry analyst has this to say concerning Xerox's new electronic publishing systems:

The electronic office is something that goes on on the other side of the screen. Out here in the real world it is beginning to look as if the paperful office will last as long as people do.

If paper is the problem and people prefer paper, perhaps the peopleless will be the next big productivity gain. (Which Computer?, November 1986, p.43)

In the office systems market the same analyst describes Xerox's performance as that of a 'sleeping giant' which has finally awakened with the introduction of a major new approach to desktop publishing based on a laser-writer that doubles as a photocopier. In its position straddling old and new technologies Xerox companies would seem to be in a uniquely favourable strategic position. However, recent performance gives cause for concern.

By any other criteria, the 33 per cent growth in office systems turnover in 1986 was a highly creditable achievement. Much less satisfactory was the level of profit earned in this expanding sector, for it is clear that, in many of the countries in which it operates, Rank Xerox derives all its profits from reprographic equipment and supplies; with business systems doing little better than break even − if that. (Foster 1987, p.65)

Foster goes on to argue that it is would be wrong to be pessimistic about the future in the new business area, although he does counsel caution. He also reminds us that, as an integral part of the 'Xerox world', Rank Xerox's fortunes are symbiotically linked to the fortunes of the whole corporation with its considerable diversity and many opportunities for revenue growth, profitability and market penetration. The copier market, though, remains of primary importance if the company is to be able to finance developments in the business systems sector (Foster 1987).

To examine the complex relations between Rank Xerox and its American parent would require another study. It is interesting to note however, how Xerox now construes the problems it came up against in the late 1970s. Many of its current managerial problems are attributed to the 'Fordist' approach to management that the company embraced in the 1960s.

When the company started getting some size ... it chose to bring in Ford people ... Ford was a monolithic, functionalized, bureaucratic, centralized organization. Belief in analysis overcomes all. ... It didn't really matter until 1975, because Xerox was the only game in town. (Jacobson and Hillkirk 1986, p.178)

The managers recruited from Ford introduced much needed management systems and financial controls but when the company's market situation changed in the late 1970s the Ford emphasis on efficiency and control was found to be at odds with the need for innovation:

we were stifled by controls. It was really holding us back. It was too well organized; it was too efficient in terms of controls and it was killing us. (Jacobson and Hillkirk 1986, p.206)

As a result a primary concern in the change process introduced in the 1980s has been re-introduce an innovatory capacity into the organisation worldwide. The philosophy of devolving control to Strategic Business Units is evolving and a major attack has been launched on the giant bureaucracy that stifled product development during the 1970s. The success of this initiative is demonstrated in the development of the 10 Series copier. The new management emphasis is on teamwork in product development in an attempt to overcome the 'turf battles', 'everyone protecting their own turf', that characterised managerial relations in the past (Jacobson and Hillkirk 1986, pp.247-8). Leadership through Quality has been used to reduce bureaucracy by examining and changing organisational processes. Leadership through Quality has also served as a mechanism for establishing faith in company performance capability. Here the role of David Kearns is crucial.

Most importantly, he recognized the necessity of getting his people to believe in the changes that were occurring. (Jacobson and Hillkirk 1986, p.316)

In production the emphasis is on the manufacture of a variety of products in the same facitility. Benchmarking has been used 'as a tool in [a] drive to lower manufacturing costs, reduce employment levels, accelerate product development and pay more attention to what the customer wants' (Jacobson and Hillkirk 1986, p.231). The biggest improvement is seen as the ability to respond more quickly to customer demand and change in the market place.

The distinctive feature of change in Rank Xerox is that it is a total process, driven by a programme extrapolated from the Fuji Xerox experience. In Rank Xerox change was, from the first, conceptualised as a total process embracing strategic choice, technical innovation in product and process, work organisation and company culture. Self-consciously drawing on Fuji Xerox practices, Rank Xerox accelerated the pervasive change process through the Leadership through Quality programme which propagated a common analytical language to maximise employee commitment to the process. It is the pervasive and ongoing nature of change in Rank Xerox which means that the organisation is in the throes of transition, an extremely fluid state whose future direction rests on the company's ability to establish a secure core market in the office systems market. As Xerox Chairman David Kearns — the architect of the Xerox change process — explains:

Xerox is clearly in a period of transition. We are no longer the company that we once were and we are not yet the company that we must be. (Xerox Corporation 1986, p.1)

The Chairman and Managing Director of Rank Xerox was equally uncompromising in his insistence in the company's 1985 International Report that the process of change had to continue:

despite these encouraging results we have no grounds for complacency. Rank Xerox is facing strong competition, depressed industry price levels, adverse currency influences and an uncertain economic environment. The key to our continued success is to establish even higher levels of activity at the same time as continuing to reduce costs.

5 Shell UK

THE PETROCHEMICAL SECTOR

The oil companies' business environment has changed markedly in the last decade and a half. The petrochemical industry, throughout the twentieth century one of the leading sectors in terms of industrial development, 'entered a new, less favourable phase in the early 1970s, marked by an accelerated erosion of the pillars sustaining its growth' (OECD 1985, p.7). A combination of factors contributed to the 'pronounced slackening in dynamism in the sector' (OECD 1985, p.7). Two oil price shocks led to a marked increase in the prices of the feedstocks that provide the industry with energy and raw materials. There was a general slowdown in economic growth. Major end use markets became saturated. The emergence on new oil exporting countries added to a growing over capacity in the industry. The 1970s and early 1980s, therefore, constituted a period of deepening crisis for the industry and if the industry has managed to emerge from this crisis it is only into a situation of continuing turbulence.

The problems facing the industry have been particularly marked in Europe. The economics of technological investment in the industry, particularly the long lead times taken for investment to mature, and the sudden and unforeseeable nature of the key events led to a failure to adjust to new market conditions. This failure to adjust was exacerbated by the failure to realise that certain trends, such as the impending saturation of major markets, were irreversible, thus generating a gradual worsening in the supply and demand imbalance caused by the first structural upheaval in the early 1970s (OECD 1985, p.7). By the early 1980s the industry found itself faced with its

worst ever crisis. Consumption fell against a background of increasing
production capacity. Capacity utilisation fell, unit production costs
rose, while, at the same time, prices fell dramatically. 1981 and 1982
were a period of serious financial loss.

There was some recovery in 1983, with a sharp recovery in demand,
cutbacks in capacity, and a tendency toward lower feedstock prices.
The effects of the rationalisation which had begun late in 1981 were
reflected in improved performances (OECD 1985, p.7). Improvement
continued through 1984, although the OECD report concludes that this
should be interpreted with caution, particularly in the light of the
industry's repeated tendency, during the 1970s, to mistake cyclical
upturns for medium-term or even long-term trends. It is especially
important for the petrochemical industry to predict these trends
accurately because of its tendency towards structural inertia, owing,
particularly, to the lengthy lead periods required for capacity
investment to mature. If trends in demand are not correctly
interpreted then serious structural imbalances can occur due to
misguided capital investment.

PROBLEMS OF MATURITY

The OECD suggests that the crisis the industry has gone through in the
last decade and a half is symptomatic of its reaching the mature stage
in it development. Maturity is evidenced by the slowdown in growth and
the increasing saturation of core markets in bulk petrochemicals.

In the foreseeable future, the tendencies detected during the past
ten years are likely to be confirmed and even intensified, since
another factor, besides the market ageing that has already been at
work for some time, will influence demand; that is lower unit
consumption in the use of certain petrochemicals in major
application (e.g. thinner plastic film for packaging). In short
... from now on, growth in total demand for bulk petrochemicals
i.e. the main thermoplastics and their precursors) is likely to
keep in step with general economic growth. (OECD 1985, p.11)

A major problem facing the industry during the 1970s and the early
1980s was the disparity between production capacity and demand. This
led to major capacity under-utilisation and the need, in the early
1980s, as the recession deepened and evidence of radical changes in
long-term demand became incontrovertible, that producers had to reduce
surplus capacity. The need to reduce capacity was further exacerbated
by the major structural change in the industry that occurred with the
development of ethane-based capacities outside traditional production
areas. This led to the creation of two major exporting 'poles' for
ethylene derivatives, namely the Middle East/North Africa and Canada.
This is leading to further market pressures on European companies and
ongoing adjustment problems of further reducing capacity and of
consolidating those business areas that demonstrate medium-term and
long-term potential competitiveness. This has led to the need to
review the forms of organisation appropriate to the industry's
changing business context.

The type of organisation that was adequate in the rapid growth phase and in a highly favourable energy context may indeed turn out to be no longer effective in the 'maturity' phase and the new supply conditions for energy products. (OECD 1985, p.13)

Readjustment possibilities include: consolidation of the sector by merger (the merging of Conoco and Du Pont in the early 1980s is a major example of this form of consolidation); the exchange of capacities between companies as a way of rationalising supply structures; and, at the level of the individual firm, changes in business strategy, perhaps the most significant of which is the expansion in the production of more specialised, higher value-added products and a trend away from the manufacture of bulk commodities. (Commodities are those undifferentiated products, including olefins such as ethylene and propylene and aromatics such as benzene, that are manufactured in bulk and sold on price rather than quality. Speciality products are manufactured in smaller amounts and include technical plastics, for example, for engineering applications, and special polymers. Their key market characteristic is quality.) There are also the major readjustment problems for the industry in the long-term of adapting to the gradual exhaustion of existing oil and gas fields and the eventual depletion of these reserves.

In the United Kingdom oil industry context, North Sea oil production looms large. Here the 'upstream' side of the oil business, that concerned with the exploration for and the extraction of oil, has experienced a recent decline in output. In 1986 annual North Sea output declined for the first time. In July 1987 daily average production figures for North Sea oil were 1.93 million barrels, the first time production had dropped below 2 million barrels per day in more than five years, evidence that the 'downtrend in North Sea production now appears firmly established' (Royal Bank/Radio Scotland Oil Index, 24 July 1987).

The problems of the industry in the North Sea illustrate the recent shift (post-1985) in profitability within the oil companies from the upstream end (exploration and production) to downstream activities (refining and marketing). It is difficult, though, to speak of a trend here as petrochemical markets are extremely volatile and price-sensitive. Thus the Financial Times (14 August 1987) commented, reporting on Royal Dutch/Shell's announcement that higher profits from oil exploration and production had been more than offset by a sharp fall in earnings from 'downstream' activities (refining and marketing):

If oil prices remained at current levels, profits from oil exploration and production would benefit, although prospects for refining and marketing remained uncertain due to competitive pressures ... [The company] suffered a squeeze on margins in oil refining ... as rising crude prices were not fully passed on in the face of fierce competition. In the comparative period last year, conditions were reversed and record profits were made.

The rise in profits in exploration and production was generated by a combination of higher oil prices and lower exploration costs. Economic and political factors are significant here with a large drop in crude oil prices in recent years reflecting both a reaction against the sharp price increases of the 1970s and a change in the political complexion of OPEC (Organisation of Petroleum Exporting Countries). As a result the oil market has shifted from scarcity to surplus, at least in the short term.

In their upstream operations competitiveness within the oil industry has focussed on the ability to 'get it out of the ground as cheaply as possible', from increasingly difficult and marginal locations, as in the North Sea. The emphasis has been on the competitive edge generated by technological innovation in drilling capability. In the downstream, technological innovation had centered on the upgrading of refineries so that they can utilise a variety of crude oils (heavy/light; high/low sulphur) to produce the highest value added products. Competitiveness had also increasingly focussed on cost effectiveness and the efficient use of manpower with consequent rationalisation. In upstream operations the collapse in the oil price and the the consequent cutback in exploration and production has had more serious employment consequences for the oil supply industry than for the oil companies themselves, which can 'offset their difficulties in exploration and production with fatter profits at the petrol pumps' (_Financial Times_, 7 November 1986). Much work in exploration and production is performed on a contractual basis and this enables oil companies to manage downturns in these activities by not renewing contracts or commencing new projects.

Downstream problems are different. Process industries are, by definition, capital-intensive, capital investment being predicated on bulk production and economies of scale. With the large increase in output of the 1960s there was a 'scaling up' of plant size, large increase in labour productivity and modest employment growth (Clark 1985). In terms of employment the problems of the 1970s and 1980s have led to a substantial shakeout of labour with, for the first time in its history, a severe employment decline (Clark 1985, p.71). The retrenchment in upstream operations and the decline in demand for downstream products, particularly plastics, has exacerbated this trend. Long-term demand prospects and, therefore, employment prospects are highly dependent on the state of major users of petrochemical products, especially in the construction, textile, automobile and packaging industries.

The locus of innovation in the industry has shifted from primarily product innovation, despite the growth in speciality markets, to primarily process innovation.

The productivity of the labour force depends on a host of factors, but over a period of a decade or so the most important are probably the state of demand for the industries' output and changing technology. (Clark 1985, pp.99-100)

The long lead times in the construction of new plant means that investment has been slow to respond to changes in demand, thus exacerbating the overcapacity problem. This has compounded the problems of rationalisation now facing the industry. Much new plant actually came on stream after the fall in demand caused by the price rises of the early 1970s 'oil shock'. Because newer capacity is more efficient and, therefore, more profitable to operate 'older plants are currently very susceptible to closure' (Clark 1985, pp.103-4). Key areas for short-term competitiveness are energy and labour costs so that innovations within these two areas are primary concerns in the harsher competitive climate of the 1980s. In downstream operations, the goal of competitive edge has been addressed particularly in the area of labour costs. Annual capital expenditure in the 1980s has declined with a marked reduction in expenditure on new projects (Clark 1985, p.106).

COMPANY PROFILE

Shell UK Limited is a company of the Royal Dutch/Shell Group. It is a fully integrated company, engaged in the exploration for and production of oil and natural gas, in oil refining and chemicals manufacturing, and in the marketing and distribution of the resulting products. The company is organised into three business sectors. Shell UK Exploration and Production (Shell Expro) explores for and produces oil and gas, primarily from the North Sea, where it is operator for the Shell/Esso joint venture. Shell UK Oil (SUKO) is responsible for the companies oil manufacturing and marketing organisation and its refineries and distribution terminals. Shell Chemicals U.K. Ltd. (SCUK) manufactures chemicals, using feedstocks supplied mainly by SUKO, and markets these and other Shell chemical products.

Thus, the company's activities can be be divided into 'upstream' and 'downstream' activities. The upstream side is responsible for the exploration for oil and its extraction. The downstream deals with the conversion of crude oil into a broad range of petroleum products, including engine fuels, most notable petroleum itself, liquified petroleum gases such as butane and propane, fuel oils for home and industry, petrochemical feedstocks, petroleum coke for industries such as steel and aluminium, and a wide variety of oils, lubricants and waxes for industrial application.

For Shell the 1980s has been a period of great change with a rapidly changing business environment imposing great pressures on the whole workforce. A former Chairman and Chief Executive, John Raisman, has described it a 'one of the most testing periods the industry has ever faced' (Annual Report, 1984). In the early 1980s pressures were particularly strong in the downstream sector due to the effects of low oil demand, a world-wide oil surplus and the resulting problems of overcapacity. As a result there was severe competition, particularly at the petrol pumps. In SUKO, refineries ran well below capacity and a constant theme of the company's operations was the pursuit of increased efficiency in adverse economic and trading environments. 1982 saw rationalisation of the company's distribution network and regional restructuring with the devolution of responsibility for managing local customers' needs to local area management. Chemicals too saw a continuing downturn in trade, after the market collapse of 1981, with low demand and consequent overcapacity and oversupply. In commodity chemicals, the currency exchange rate was a key factor with a strong pound making it difficult to export to Europe and to compete with imports. For SUKO, there was the exchange problem of the pound declining in value against a strong dollar, thus increasing the cost burden.) The need to reduce overcapacity led to job losses, particularly at Stanlow, Shell's main chemical manufacturing site, in all areas including management and engineering support services. In contrast to the problems in commodity chemicals, speciality chemicals saw sustained demand and were relatively unaffected by the recession. The growing importance of the speciality end of the market was demonstrated by opening of the Shell Higher Olefins Process plant at Stanlow, the only one of its kind in Europe. This produces the base material for a wide range of speciality chemicals.

1983 saw a continuing pressure on the manufacturing and marketing side of the business and on chemicals, a situation characterised by the company as one of 'production strength and market weakness' (Annual Report, 1983). In the refineries the main goal continued to be the increase of output in higher value products. The company reported that it was paying particular attention to organisational issues, particularly the management of change.

Another area to which we have been devoting increasing attention has been the management of change. The challenge of ever keener competition, as well as of the shifting pattern of demand in many parts of the business, requires us to make a continuous effort to improve the structure of the Company and its operational efficiency. (Annual Report, 1983)

A key factor emphasised in this process of self-analysis and improvement was the support and cooperation of employees. In the generation of this support and cooperation communication as the basis of employee involvement was stressed. A central theme of the company's employee relations policy was communication, with an ongoing 'Cascade' exercise to inform the workforce about the the business environment and the rationale behind company strategy. All staff were involved in face-to-face discussions with management about the company's problems and plans.

In SUKO the business environment continued to be characterised by surpluses and overcapacity and the decisive competitive factor was cost effectiveness. Three key areas were signalled out: investment to make plants more efficient; reorganisation to achieve higher productivity; and the need to align employee numbers with the levels required to operate efficiently. Refineries were upgraded to allow the production of greater volumes of more valuable lighter products for which demand remained strong. The company's upgrading capacity was increased by more than 10 per cent in 1983 and the extra capacity was being fully utilised by the end of the year. In chemicals the company began a period of 'climb-back' after the 'bottoming-out' at the end of 1982. SCUK benefited from reductions in plant capacity and manning levels to make considerable steps in a return to competitiveness with the most efficient Western European plants.

During the first half of the 1980s, while downstream businesses struggled, upstream operations went from strength to strength. It was the rising contribution from its North Sea operations that permitted the company to remain profitable.

The contrasting fortunes of the oil industry were clearly apparent in Shell UK's 1984 results. For the exploration and production side of the business it was an outstanding year, while for the oil manufacturing and marketing sector the growing strength of the dollar against the pound pushed up supply costs and made the struggle for profitability harder than ever. (Annual Report, 1984)

For the first time since its inception in 1976, the downstream oil business (SUKO) recorded an operating loss in 1984. Due to the collapse in demand for its main product, gas oil for heating, with little prospect of sustained recovery in the long-term, the company announced the closure of its Teesport Refinery with consequent redundancies. A considerable reduction in manpower was also announced at Stanlow Refinery as the company set about further restructuring and streamlining in the search of profitability in, at best, static markets.

Rationalisation of jobs continued in the pursuit of efficiency. By the end of the year, at the Shell Haven refinery, for example, manning levels had been halved by the end of 1984 from their 1981 levels. At SUKO head office, an analysis of manning and activity levels started in 1983, was completed in 1984 with a 28 per cent reduction in manpower. The number of employees in Shell UK fell during 1984 by 5 per cent to 16,675. Reflecting the relative prosperity of the upstream side of the business, numbers employed in Shell Expro rose 7 per cent. Positive gains, though, were made in the chemicals sector with SCUK achieving a virtual breakeven position after a four year period of losses. The future for chemicals looked brighter because the company now enjoyed a technological edge over its competitors, by virtue of of its half share in production from the new ethane cracker at Mossmoran and the new higher olefins plant at Stanlow.

1985 marked a turnaround in the company's business position. The new Chairman and Chief Executive, Robert Reid, reported:

Nineteen eighty-five was a year of significant achievements in all three business sectors of Shell UK and these are reflected in our improved results. (Annual Report, 1985)

Oil and chemicals manufacturing and marketing returned to cost-competitiveness, while restructuring in these areas was continued to build on renewed cost-competitiveness. The Chairman signalled out 'a new commitment and realism' on the part of employees that had permitted necessary changes, for example, in the area of more flexible approaches to work, to be implemented. The greater understanding between management and employees at the local level was emphasised as a significant change factor. With this improved quality of employee relations, a major programme of investment was announced for downstream operations. A key problem facing the company remained 'the question of sustaining momentum of development in the face of price uncertainties' (Annual Report, 1985). Particularly significant for the future was the increasing turbulence of international crude oil prices and currency exchange markets, with ominous signs, in early 1986, of dramatic falls in crude oil prices. This led, in 1986 and 1987, to a loss of jobs in Shell Expro.

The decline in crude oil prices means benefits in cost reductions for the manufacturing, supply and marketing, downstream, side of the business. 1985 saw a major improvement in refinery performance as the benefits of the previous years' restructuring and investment programs began to work their way through. These were reinforced by further actions to cut overcapacity and reduce costs, leading to considerable productivity improvements. A major initiative in this area was the announcement of a reduction in the 3,300 combined oil and chemicals workforce at Stanlow Refinery by 1000. The restructuring of work practices led to further productivity improvements. In Chemicals, particularly at the Carrington plant, there were major changes in both operations and working practices during 1985. The rationalisation of the Company's business according to a policy of devolving responsibility to separate, fully accountable business units continued with the setting up of Shell Gas to be responsible for the running of the company's liquified gas business and the development of Shell Lubricants UK, responsible for the lubricating oil business, within SUKO.

CHANGES IN WORK ORGANISATION AT SHELL UK

The problems facing the management of Shell UK's downstream operations are encapsulated in the following statement by Peter Brown, manager of Stanlow Refinery.

> Demand for oil products in the UK has dropped by 35 per cent over the past ten years and is most unlikely to rise. Both the oil manufacturing and marketing sector, and the chemicals sector, of Shell UK are not earning their keep. (Financial Times, 7 March 1985).

This drastic situation called for drastic remedies. This section examines the changes introduced in work organisation in the downstream side of Shell's business. Shell Chemicals provided the prototype for the kind of changes the company has aimed for in the second half of the 1980s. The prime exemplar of these changes is the Carrington Chemical Plant which has seen major changes in both operations and working practices since 1985.

Carrington's losses were the major factor in Shell Chemicals' UK deficit in the 1980s. New capital investment 'narrowed the product base required from Carrington' (IDS Report 453, 1985, p.2). The newly constructed Mossmoran Esso/Shell plant made the production of ethylene at Carrington uneconomic. Rationalisation of production at Carrington focussed on the production of products considered to have continuing viability in an increasingly hostile business environment. The plant's naptha-based ethylene cracker, together with the ethylene oxide and ethylene glycol plants, were closed down and feedstocks feedstock provided from the new ethylene plant. Operations at Carrington were concentrated on the production of plastics.

The survival plan drawn up for Carrington was made contingent upon the halving of the workforce. Fundamental operational and organisational changes were introduced, marking a major break with past traditions of job demarcation, and the pursuit of a 'leaner, fitter' organisation. Two of the six organisational layers between the site manager and the operators were removed. The three separate agreements covering process, craft and staff have been replaced by a single salaried 'technician' grade which covers all employees including administrative staff. Craft demarcations have been replaced by the 'Carrington technician' with a move from a 'traditional' grading structure to a single salaried grade of 'fully flexible shift technician' (IDS Report 453, 1985, p.3). Craftsmen and operators have become fully flexible shift technicians. The various craft groups have been amalgamated into 4 trade groups: instrument/electrical; moving equipment; static equipment; and civil. Demarcation have been abolished within these groups so that, for example engineering and electrical work can be performed by either electrician or engineers interchangeably. Every technician is expected to perform any work which he has the knowledge to perform safely.

The new 'multi-skilled' technician replaces craftsmen and operators. The technicians function as integrated teams able to perform each others' jobs and to carry our a broad range of operating and maintenance work. To facilitate the new role special training units were established to develop the flexibility required. The Carrington agreement also allows for the increased use of contract labour. The streamlined craft workforce will handle the core of refinery maintenance while contractors are used for peak work loads and non-core refinery activities. Contractors are to be used for a range of engineering related activities and for plant cleaning, plate laying, lagging and civil works (IDS Report 453, 1985, p.3). As a consequence of these changes manpower at Carrington has been reduced from 1,200 to 500. Changes in working practices and the acceptance of rationalisation were accompanied by improved pay for the remaining workforce. The company described itself as 'lean not mean'.

These changes reflect the adaptation of the company at the level of work organisation to the demands of a market where the major competitive factor was lower costs. A major communications exercise to support the changes at Carrington, using employee briefings, leaflets and videos, was based on the premise that 'the "new" Carrington is effectively a greenfield site with complete flexibility of labour' (IDS Report 455, 1985, p.5). (The new Mossmoran plant operates with a fully flexible workforce.) The company did not, however, seek a single union agreement and continued to recognise four unions, the TGWU, ASTMS, AUEW and EETPU, for collective bargaining purposes. For accepting the changes substantial pay increases, totalling 32 per cent over a two year period, were agreed.

Carrington served as template for change in the rest of Shell's downstream operations. The key 'concept', pioneered at Carrington and then diffused throughout the company, was based on the principle of 'breaking down old demarcations and moving into multi-skilling territory'. Similar moves towards flexibility, manpower rationalisation and the simplification of grading structures have been made at Stanlow refinery with a move from 20 craft trades to three categories of operative: fabrication, fitting, and power and control with flexibility within and between the three categories. Craftsmen are now required to be flexible in the performance of the work of each of the trades within their trade group and to 'tackle the work of the other groups where they have the time, tools and ability' (IDS Report 459, 1985, p.3). At Stanlow there is not the same breaking down of the barrier between craftsman and operator achieved at Carrington although there had been a weakening of the boundaries between the two groups. Process operators work has been reorganised on a team basis, and teams have responsibility for a wider range of work including certain maintenance functions. The Stanlow agreement, like that at Carrington, also includes a core maintenance policy with the use of contractors for peak work loads and non-core maintenance work. There is to be a reduction of the workforce at Stanlow from 3,300 to 2,300 over a two year period. In line with the changes introduced as part of the Carrington productivity agreement, there has also been decentralisation of staff bargaining throughout the downstream side of the business (IDS Report 465, 1986, p.3).

On the distribution side pay restructuring has also focussed on the need for greater flexibility with a new agreement that

requires that employees cooperate fully in: flexibility of working practices both within and across job categories; acceptance and maintenance of agreed national performance standards; shift and rota working which is compatible with the company's operational requirements; and the elimination of wasted time and all restrictive practices. (IDS Report 488, 1987, p.13)

The alternative offered the drivers was a contracting out of the distribution operation, something other oil industry firms have already done. In return for the acceptance of the changes Shell guaranteed investment in a new tanker fleet and a new computer system. The company was unequivocal in its explaining of the basis for this new investment.

This investment cannot be made without fundamental changes in the way we do things. Our investment must be put to work properly. (Financial Times, 11 November 1986)

The company did, as part of the deal increase its use of non-core labour in distribution, with contractors increasing their share carriage from 12 to 25 per cent of oil volume. In return for the changes in working practices and a reduction of around one-third of the workforce there has been a pay rise of 33 per cent.

There have been similar developments in Shell's upstream operations, Shell Expro. Here the new emphasis is on the development of multi-skilled operating technicians for work on North Sea oil platforms. The move is away from a rigid separation of work according to a 'craft-type individual on the engineering side and a process-type individual on the process side' to the principle of one kind of flexible technician covering both these roles. The rationale here is again economic.

The prime mover for us in Northern Waters is cost in that to be more efficient, given that it costs so much to take a man out there and keep him out there, we [aim to] utilise their potential to the full.

The model for this sort of change has been operations in Southern Waters gas fields where flexible working has become the norm for similar efficiency reasons. There are implications for the organisation of management in this sort of development, primarily 'a need for structural re-examination' concerning the need to keep separate operations and engineering management structures. The company has questioned whether it needs 'distinct disciplines' and one result has been that installation managers on off-shore platforms have been made 'totally and fully responsible'.

Functionally, previously, engineering reported to people on-shore and the managers were process man.

THE MANAGEMENT OF CHANGE

Pressures for change have been different in different parts of the business. This is illustrated by the differences between Stanlow and Carrington.

Stanlow was coming at it from a totally different direction, i.e., not under the same business pressure as Carrington. Carrington had an option. It either changed or it closed. Stanlow did not. Stanlow had the only business pressure, the one that we would normally recognise, that it needed to be more efficient and more productive, but there was no threat of closure. If anything the only significant threat hanging over Stanlow was that if they didn't improve their general productivity levels and come into line with European refinery standards or, more particularly, our Dutch ones, they might not get any new investment. We didn't say they'd die but that they simply wouldn't be renewed, they might begin to cut back a bit.

Dutch refineries efficiency edge was attributed to the consequences of demarcations in the UK and also the UK higher ratio of indirect to direct workers. Carrington demonstrated to the company what was possible in terms of changing working practices. It served as a 'good model'.

Carrington was necessary to make the system realise that certain things could be done, and, to that extent, it was very useful that Carrington broke the first sods, if you like, and started a new process going in manufacturing, but the refineries were very close behind, following.

The key problem the company found it necessary to address was a skill problem compounded by a problem of productivity. The background to changed in working practices is addressed by Michael Cross.

As part of cost cutting exercises companies have reduced their numbers of engineering craftsmen and introduced varying degrees of flexibility amongst those remaining. Even in our low wage economy, old working practices are no longer affordable. On the technical side, the introduction of new plant and equipment embodying the latest technologies is creating needs for both a multi-disciplinary and a systems approach to fault-finding and maintenance work. The old single discipline based approach offered by most engineering craftsmen is becoming increasingly inappropriate. (Cross 1985, p.viii)

The dominant business need now in chemical and oil refining industries is for cross-traded engineering craftsmen with a broad range of core mechanical and instrument/electrical skills. In terms of the craftsmen's role, the need is for them to take greater responsibility and work with reduced supervision. This need is 'related to the need for rapid identification, diagnosis and rectification of faults on the plant' (Cross 1985, p.69). The major production imperative in highly capital intensive process plants is to prevent stoppages in production. An increase in responsibility also reduces the costs of supervision. At Carrington the old shift foreman grade has been removed in the new slimmed-down organisational structure. On the process side, too, for the same economic and technological reasons, there is a need to update skills and move to combined maintenance and production operators' jobs.

What is evolving is a new

multi-role way of working covering a wide range of tasks which would be traditionally termed skilled and unskilled, and also maintenance and production tasks. This calls into question both the craft-assistance and craft-process/production interfaces. (Cross 1985, p.90)

The combining of decision-making, technical and other forms of knowledge with small group autonomy and responsibility for their actions also calls into question the labour-management interface.

The problems still facing the company are illustrated by what one manager describes as 'our most interesting new working practices'. These are taking shape in Shell UK Oil at its new lubricants blending and packaging facility at Stanlow, Shell Lubricants Centre Stanlow (SLCS). This plant, the most modern integrated lubricating oil processing, blending and distribution operation in Europe, represents a significant technological advance. It is manned by people 'coming out of very old-fashioned working environments'. Therefore it requires a major change of attitude, not only in the workforce but also in management. SLCS has used Carrington as a model for its 'flattened hierarchical system' – 'it's a very flat structure' – and for its new technician grade. The working environment differs from Carrington in its state of the art technology but its workforce is drawn from similar working traditions. Carrington, therefore, has also provides a model of the kinds of new attitudes to work that need to be developed.

The skill base, though, differs from Carrington's.

It's different in the sense that Carrington is much more geared to the interchangeability of operational and craft skill, much more geared to the idea of operators doing their own maintenance on the plant, because it's a process plant of a different kind. We're not talking in that sense at SLCS. There it's the acquisition of more skills to do a wider range of jobs on the plant, not craft skills but operational skills. Carrington is a little more geared to what people understand in terms of crossing boundaries, picking up other unions' skills. We're not talking about that at SLCS because the whole craft maintenance side is different.

The immediate issue, then, is the training of the workforce in a new range of skills:

if you make drastic changes in work organisation in terms of multi-skilling and so on it makes a terrific demand on you in terms of training load. It frequently gets under-estimated.

A key company goal is to deal with the tradition of

people working in departments ... operating in compartments ... to break down much of that compartmentalisation ... you're in a situation where you're breaking down some of the barriers that were dividing them.

The progression in this direction is a gradual one. Stanlow illustrates this.

They've moved considerably from where they were and, although they haven't yet broken down the final barrier between the craftsman and the operator they've certainly diminished it and there's much more passage between them, as there is between blue-collar and white-collar. So they've already moved into a much more flexible, multi-flexible system than they previously had.

The over-riding managerial imperative in developing this flexibility was the need to communicate with the workforce concerning the new situation facing the company.

We had to communicate much more widely, much more deeply, with the workforce. We talked to the unions and the shopfloor, explaining the nature of the business, problems with the business, what we were doing about it, letting them have their say, trying to get it across that we were all in it together and trying to get the best result. That was absolutely essential.

The central aim was the generation of mutual trust via direct communication with the labour force building on 'a record of being open and honest.' This was construed as a battle to win the hearts and minds of the workforce.

We took a conscious decision decision as a personnel policy that we would set out not just to inform and communicate but to actually win the hearts and minds of our employees as a conscious effort by management to ensure that the business would be run more

96

effectively. Even if the news was bad we felt it was absolutely crucial that people ought to understand.

The prime example of this approach was Carrington.

We were absolutely blunt, very, very frank. It was the only way to get the message across.

We took a conscious decision that we would communicate direct, not indirect. No way were we going to do it through the unions. It was much too important. It was our responsibility to make sure there was proper understanding. You're seeking the agreement of your own employees, managing with their consent. You're trying to mobilise employee consent and you can't do that through the unions. It's not the unions' role to explain to our employees what the business is all about. It's not their business to win their hearts and minds, the consensus of the workforce, as management is seeking to do.

The alternative was the 'abdication of managerial responsibility'.

Despite the fact that 'the unions never wanted to admit that it was all necessary', the need for change was accepted by the workforce, despite union resistance and calls for strike action which the workforce refused.

The result was that because people understood the nature of the problems they accepted the necessity of change. This was shown in a very sad way. On three separate occasions the union national officials called the men to come out on strike and three times they were told to get lost.

Underpinning all these changes has been a new company emphasis on commitment to results and an 'ideology' entitled 'the customer is king'. There is an ongoing commitment to improving performance and a new stress on quality. Following a similar ideology to that underpinning quality circles, there has been a move, developed at Carrington and also developing at Stanlow, in upstream operations, and an intrinsic part of the new system at SLCS, of operators taking on their own quality control work.

Instead of, as previously had been the pattern, having samples taken by lab technicians and taken away for testing, now the operators do that themselves, so they've got this much greater commitment to the quality in the sense that they're doing their own testing and sampling. To that extent we've developed those sort of ideas which are not far from the quality circle sort of idea. It's much more immediate, much more upfront, and they're qualified to do it, they've got the skills to do it. They sometimes need a bit of training about the techniques but they've no skills problem.

Management, too, has had to change. With the reduction in levels of management

> you get much more hands-on management, you get people actually more involved with the process they're actually responsible for, people who are prepared to cross boundaries as well so they themselves are much more flexible. Also they are much more business-orientated. They actually understand and follow through the linkages between their own activity and the impact on the business.

The company stresses that individual plant managers are now their own industrial relations managers with negotiation devolved to the local level. There is a 'similarity in style and approach' at the different plants but the elements of the various agreements struck at the local level differ.

> We've deliberately been fostering difference. ... The more differences we've got the more the people locally can gear what they've got to what they need.

Personnel's role, therefore, has changed to one of facilitation of local management thinking and helping in local thinking and, more importantly, to making the company generally responsive to overall business needs in its personnel policies. Personnel, as a result, has itself become 'much, much more aware of its business involvement'.

> Key areas of change in management include the need to give up its own 'demarcations'.

> People have to forget some of their own demarcations. So a production manager, for example, doesn't just sit blinkered and worry about production. He's got to worry about 'O.K., what's the impact on the other bit of the business?' The maintenance man the same, the lab man the same. They themselves have got to get out of their old rather insular style.

Management, too, like the workforce in its adaptation to new patterns of work organisation, has to learn the value of teamwork. This is illustrated by the experience of the management team responsible for the planning of the new Stanlow Lubricants plant.

> The management teams need to develop, working together rather than working separately. The SLCS management team went off [recently], an offsite week somewhere in Wales, and did all sorts of apparently crazy things. A very necessary week, because they needed to gell together. They certainly weren't gelling at one stage. One or two of them were building all sorts of barriers to these new ideas that were beginning to be advanced for the workforce. 'Can't manage that, can't handle that. We need this, we nee the other.' And it was all drawn from their own experiences. They weren't looking at it from the totality of the operations of the plant. They were just looking at it from their own 'Can't

handle that.' So that week away was necessary to get them to break down some of those sorts [of thinking).

The team-development approach depended on the inputs of the Shell organisation development (OD) group. It was 'very much an OD inspired and OD driven activity'. The OD group plays a key role in the change process in the company, a role that we will analyse in the following section.

The roots of the problem of managerial 'compartmental' thinking lie partly in allegiance to technical specialism, because the managers involved are by definition technical people, and also in traditional routine approaches to work organisation rather than technical myopia per se.

[Managers] are people who have mostly been working in a particular environment for quite a longish time. Any body in that environment thinks their own function is better and can get blinkered.

The vital role of leadership in the change process was singled out.

How has it [the introduction of new work organisation] been approached from the management side? Often, by very clear and direct leadership from some significant member of management. There's no doubt about it that the Carrington experience was driven top down. The key figure in that was the managing director and he was driving Chemicals to look at new things and to develop new [approaches]. The same thing is happening at Stanlow Refinery, for example. That's being driven largely by two men, the manufacturing director [at central headquarters] and the refinery manager on site. Those two people have enough vision about where they want to be and the things they want to achieve that they drive the system to adapt and to find ways of improving.

The leadership supplies the vision and the impetus to change. The problem is then one of translating this strategic vision into widespread action. Here Organisation Development (OD) consultants – internal and external – play a key role.

ORGANISATION DEVELOPMENT

Shell has a long tradition of using organisation development (OD) personnel to solve its organisational problems. The OD group is deeply involved in the implementation of the change processes primarily in its role of facilitating new ways of thinking about the implementation of solutions to the problems facing the company. A major change arena has been that of altering managerial attitudes to adapt to the new business demands and the new more flexible approaches to work that changes in these demands have brought in their train.

It requires a change of attitude of a fairly significant kind. Now there's a lot of work invested, starting with the management of that [the SLCS] plant and getting them to change attitudes and style. That's being driven very strongly by one individual but with the help of OD people. A number of consultants are working [at] setting up a training module, setting up the job design, setting up a change of attitudes on the part of management. It is not only the plant operators who have got to change. The managers have got to change. They're bringing with them a whole host of the old baggage and the old style.

OD's role is seen as a key support role once the need for change has been flagged by a key individual. The leadership supplies the vision and the impetus to change. OD consultants, either Shell's own internal consultants or external consultants brought in with specific skills, are then used to generate ways of helping in the implementation of the change process as, for example, in the team—building at Stanlow.

As far as SLCS is concerned they [the OD consultants] have been vital to getting the management thinking right for handling the changes that are important for making SLCS successful, and they've been playing a vital role. Without them it wouldn't be happening. They've played a vital role in that process.

OD is a very important bit of the business and we use it very extensively on all fronts. ... Once you've got someone driving towards change, then the OD boys come into their own because they are extremely valuable as facilitators of that change, once somebody is driving them. They can very rarely initiate it, they can offer thoughts up, but they're very rarely in the position, or wish to be for that matter, of saying, 'Come on, let's do it.' What they're around for and are very good at is providing the vehicles and the processes for handling and initiating change once somebody has wanted it to get there. But you need that desire and that intention to get there first. All my experience over the years with the OD people is that they are marvellous as facilitators but they're not really the best people for initiating something. Indeed , that puts them in the wrong position because that begins to destroy their objectivity.

OD's role is to maintain the impetus of the change program by dealing with 'soft, human' problems. OD's importance lies

on the soft side of the change program, which, on the hard side, is to do with, for example, negotiating with trade unions about new working practices. The OD unit, in essence, has been helping management to handle the change programme.

OD is very much strategy—orientated. OD activities 'flow from the corporate strategy'. OD consultants work with 'key influence people' to help them manage the change process.

Shell has a long history of using OD but its current approach to the area differs form earlier approaches. A new style of OD with a central focus on strategy has replaced what is now described as Shell's 'difficult experience' with OD in the late '60s and early '70s.

It was quite painful in a number of places. It was a different style of OD from that which is currently the generality in the

100

Shell system now. It was much more interventionist and much more up-front, and, because of that, for about 5 years afterwards it was very much in decline. It was almost a dirty word. You mentioned OD and people shied away because there had been some very unfortunate experiences from it. Since then they've adopted a very different stance. Our senior OD consultant refuses almost to talk about OD anymore and much prefers organisational effectiveness as a title. OD still has that baggage from way back, to some extent, the old Californian style, T-groups, sensitivity training, and all that, which caused a lot of problems.

The change is to a use of OD as an adjunct to the process of pursuing business aims not just as an end in itself. OD services are brought in to facilitate the ongoing process of change.

The important point is that our OD people, when they establish a contract it means with whoever the driving force is in this particular process of change. It's very clear that their client is whoever it is.

The approach is more strategic than formerly and more eclectic. The OD consultants do not

pedal a particular line of OD ... They don't say 'The answer to everything is to do team-building' or 'The answer to everything is to do T-groups'.

The new strategic OD first proved itself in its contribution to team-building for project teams in the North Sea, improving project groups effectiveness in 'bringing in' gas/oil finds on time, thus making a significant financial contribution to the business. This gave the approach renewed legitimacy in the company. OD had to be seen to be

making a real contribution to the effectiveness of the business. The balance sheet was the hard bottom line. If we couldn't convince them that we could improve the bottom-line result there'd be no long-term commitment. [They needed to know] it wasn't only about satisfaction at work and nice things like that, that it was about long-term profitability.

OD had to show it was not just 'nice. soft, cuddly'. The success with project team development demonstrated OD's potential.

We were seen to be relevant and useful to busy line managers. They really started to appreciate what the human sciences might be able to contribute to their work.

Underlying the changes in work organisation and the emphasis on OD as a key tool for facilitating change is the search for a new organisational responsiveness in a fast changing business environment.

What is important is designing a flexible organisation with a much more involved workforce. We were trying to say we could no longer have rigid hierarchies, bosses, subordinates, trying to ensure that we involved employees. First, in helping them to think through what they were doing, what their section or department was doing. Second, trying to enable them, with management, to come to better solutions as to how the work could best be achieved.

CONCLUSION

The late 1970s and the 1980s have seen major changes in the oil industry, particularly major fluctuations in the price of oil and major changes in staple petrochemical products. This has been most dramatically manifested in the collapse of the bulk chemical market. At the strategic level these changes in product markets led to moves to reduce dependence on bulk commodities and to develop a portfolio of more specialised petrochemical products and, thus, more profitable long-term specialist businesses – 'specialty products that are difficult to imitate on short notice and fetch high prices per unit of quantity because of their greater utility to the customers whose special needs they meet' (Sabel 1982, p.208). The shift in emphasis to speciality products also necessitates a new emphasis on quality rather than price as a key marketing factor. This has led to moves to increase quality awareness in the company.

The continuing importance of the commodity business is to provide the positive cash flow to enable the development of higher technology, more specialised higher value-added products. Exacerbating the problems of adapting to this form of change are the oscillating fortunes of the upstream and downstream sides of the business. In attempts to develop business opportunities not at the mercy of economic cycles and fragile political in the late 1970s saw the cash-rich oil companies trying to diversify, 'keen to get closer to the consumer and away from low value-added commodities' (Financial Times, 18 June 1986). The key managerial concern in the oil business during the 1980s has been the concentration on the improvement of efficiency.

The change process has been driven by a logic of efficiency. The demands of efficiency have led to major rationalisation of manpower and a consequent need to use remaining employees as effectively as possible. This latter need has been met by moves towards flexibility of working practices, an upgrading of operator skills and a restructuring of craft work, plus a more flexible approach to management manifested in the attack on managerial hierarchies. At the production level the nature of process industry technology has also required a certain kind of worker due to

the growing importance ... of engineering an active vigilance, responsibility and initiative among workers ... as a result of the increasing integration, interdependency and capital intensity of the production process. (Elger 1982, p.49)

Shell management has responded to the demands of remaining competitive by emphasising the importance of developing cooperative employee relations. It is particularly important in the process industries to develop employee relations strategies that will help reduce downtime to a minimum in this highly capital intensive industry. The industry demands high skill levels. Indeed, according to Shell management, an important factor facilitating the change process in the company has been the generally positive attitude to change of their employees.

The other thing that one can't lose sight of is that, by and large, in companies like ours, we employ highly intelligent and articulate people. Our operators are not labourers by any stretch of the imagination. Most of them are pretty well qualified, they've got technical qualifications of some kind or another. So you're talking about a very, very bright bunch of people who are quite aware of what is happening in a business sense to the company and are quite aware of what the pressures are and how to handle them. So when you're dealing with issues such as, 'Fellows, it's a case of closure or else at Carrington,' or, 'Fellows, at Stanlow it's either a case of us improving our productivity ratios or else we're not going to get any more investment for a new cracker or whatever', you're pushing an open door. It's not an intransigent attitude ... it's a very responsive attitude. Sometimes it can be bloody-minded, of course, if we get it wrong and play it badly, but you're dealing with intelligent people who understand these things and, sometimes, are ahead of the game on some of these issues. So in terms of changing attitudes you're pushing against a very, very easily opened door because they, themselves, often want to play that game.

The emphasis is on consensus management. At the same time the general management style may be described, in the term used in a study of a chemical factory, as 'modern' — 'open and informative, but it is also hard and assertive' (Marchington and Parker 1987, p.14). There is, obviously, a tension between consensus and assertiveness, a tension reflected in the need to develop a committed workforce and the need for rationalisation. Working in more committed, efficient manner can be seen to lead to possible job loss. Blackler and Brown suggest that demanning at Shell in the the 1960s served to 'demolish'

the tradition of loyalty to the company which had provided a form of motivation, a sense of obligation to do a fair day's work. (Blackler and Brown 1980, p.31).

Shell management has learnt from hard experience the value of an incremental approach to change building on foundations and processes that have already been established. Shell's preoccupation with change goes back to the Shell New Philosophy of Management (Flanders 1964). The New Philosophy sought to change the Shell employee relations culture from one of competition to one of cooperation, from authoritarian-paternalistic to consensual (Blackler and Brown 1980). The philosophy emphasised the joint optimisation of social and technical systems through the creation of

conditions in which employees at all levels will be encouraged and enabled to develop and to realise their potentialities while contributing to the Company's objectives. (Blackler and Brown 1980, p.171)

The technology demanded a high level of personal responsibility and initiative among employees. The key problem in highly capital-intensive process industries

> is to avoid lapses of attention and errors in observing, diagnosing and communicating for acting upon information. Information handling work in the refining industry is such that lapses and errors are likely to result in heavy costs, both from delay in recognising errors and taking corrective action and from the nature of the equipment and the processes involved. The only promising way to avoid these faults is for the individual to be <u>internally</u> motivated to exercise responsibility and initiative. Any <u>external</u> control can only act after the error has occurred or has its effect. (Blackler and Brown 1980, p.175)

A primary need, therefore, was to develop commitment by involving employees in their work. Jobs were redesigned to increase personal commitment and responsibility and to involve individuals in decision-making. Job design also recognised individual needs for social support through an emphasis on teamwork and the need for recognition.

Interpretations of the success of the New Philosophy differ but recent analyses suggest that it was not a lasting success (Blackler and Brown 1980). A manager who had been actively involved in the 'new philosophy' initiative reflected on why he felt it had failed and also on what he thought the company had learnt from it.

> The Philosophy? The main reason that failed is ... well two reasons. One is management commitment. It was heavily associated with two or three particular individuals, one of whom retired, and the guy who replaced him didn't have the same commitment, because it wasn't built into the criteria of selection for who should do the damn job. Nowadays I hope we would say, 'Whoever comes into that job must maintain the continuity of that programme.' And the other thing is, we were too green, we didn't know how to use it. I think now we're much better at translating OD concepts into practical action. You have to go through a learning process. I don't criticise people for being green because that's just how it is. When you first get into something you don't know and you have to learn by experience. But it's a pity. What came out of it really was an education process, a seeding process really. That's putting it at its lowest. But in terms of what was a very ambitious programmes it' unrecognisable, the concepts ... You can't walk into Stanlow Refinery or Shell Haven now and say, 'Yes, I can see it in action.' It's got subsumed in other things.

Yet, in the more recent change programmes there are distinct continuities with the the principles underpinning the New Philosophy of the 1960s, particularly in the emphasis on involving employees in the process of change.

> It's growing. It started with the company philosophy, had its ups and downs, but, basically, it was up the whole time. The whole thing about employee involvement has been growing stronger since

the Sixties and it's still there. So it's a culture of participation.

What seems to have changed in the company's more recent attempts to introduce changes that are at least as radical and far-reaching is that the company has managed to synchronise its change agents' activity and market needs. The changes in the OD function exemplify this process as it has become more strategic. The changes reflect a cultural change. The company has become, as one OD activist put it, 'much leaner, hungrier, and quote "business-oriented", unquote'. It has also become 'much more flexible.'

Some of the steps in the hierarchy were removed. A much flatter organisation. Too many layers has people creating work and that just had to go.

The foci of change have been flexibility and communication to develop employee commitment.

The most important is improved flexibility in ways which get the work done with a greater sense of commitment from the workforce for the benefit of the bottom line.

A key factor facilitating change has been OD, a fact reflected in its growing involvement in the corporate planning process — 'the whole process of how do you go about the business'.

We hadn't been previously involved in that sort of fundamental issue of well-being of the company. It was only in the peripheral sense of whether or not Joe Bloggs' job was enriched or whatever. You didn't have the chance to do anything worthwhile.

The emphasis here is

to ensure that it [the company approach to corporate planning] was the most effective method, that all relevant things are taken into consideration in that plan. Is it just mechanistic, financial and technical calculation or does it involve the people side of things as well? How do you involve the people side in those calculations?

The ongoing attempt to answer these questions reflects the company's determination to move from a reactive, crisis mode of management to a more proactive, strategic mode. It reflects the goal of optimising both technical and social possibilities (Cross 1985, p.118).

New working practices stress employee flexibility and cooperation and emphasise the nature of teamwork. This is something managers too have to foster in their dealings with each other. The need for cooperation reaches from top to bottom of an organisation.

The top team of an organisation, if it is to achieve quality and commitment in its decisions about future directions, will need to pool the full extent of each individual's wisdom and experience. That means something quite different from reacting to a problem in terms of their own functional knowledge and experience. It means

exposing fully their uncertainties, taking unaccustomed risks by
airing their own subjective view of the world and struggling to
build some common perceptions and possibilities. (Critchley and
Casey 1984, p.166)

It requires a transition that the experience of most organisations
makes difficult to contemplate.

Most functional executives, brought up in the hurly-burly of
politics and inter-functional warfare, find the transition from
functional to strategic mode very difficult to make. They do not
always see the difference, and if they do, they are reluctant to
leave their mountain top, the summit of knowledge, experience and
hence power, for the equality and shared uncertainty of strategic
decision making. And yet this is on area where real teamwork is
not only necessary but vital. (Critchley and Casey 1984, p.166)

A key problem, one Shell should appreciate better than most given
their experience with the New Philosophy of management, is the problem
of sustaining the momentum of change. Here the key factor seems to be
management attitude and that changes in working practices are
accompanied by changes in organisational climate. One way of
construing the OD initiative at Shell is that it is primarily
concerned with the aligning of organisational climate with new
strategic directions and with ensuring that the organisation does not
resist change.

Learning from experience often means learning from pain. This aspect
of the change process is poignantly expressed by one senior Shell
executive reflecting on his experience of attempts to change the
company during the last two decades.

Hopefully, we've learnt our lesson now. If you look at the history
of this sort of thing since Alan Flanders and the Fawley Blue
Book, we've all been around the course two or three times and
every time we do it we say 'Yes, this time it's going to be
different'. I think we actually edge forward a bit each time but
it's a long painful process. I joined Shell having read Alan
Flanders' book and what Shell said they were going to do in the
productivity bargaining business and I thought 'Terrific, let's
get into something trail-blazing.' And it was, at the time. We all
thought it was the new millenium, but, as I say, we've been round
the course two or three times since.

6 Conclusion

The debate about organisational responses to economic crisis has primarily focussed on the need for strategic and structural realignment. Work organisation is rarely considered as an integral element of competitive strategy. Both ongoing shifts in the contours of previously stable mass markets and radical product and process innovation demand profound organisational change to maintain competitiveness. In this context maintaining or regaining competitive advantage is critically dependent upon striking an optimal balance between maximising the productivity and versatility of work organisation, reconciling — however temporarily — the innovation-efficiency dilemma.

In this study we have examined the impetus, dynamics and impact of pervasive change processes in four contrasting organisations, Ford, Pilkington, Rank Xerox, and Shell. Pilkington and Shell relied primarily upon existing managerial expertise to devise and implement their change strategies, although the latter had a powerful organisation development tradition which provided the intellectual framework for current initiatives. By contrast, Ford U.K. and Rank Xerox drew vital conceptual elements of their change agendas from Japan and their organisational links with their American parent company. Nevertheless, despite the manifold differences in the change strategies adopted by the four organisations we conclude that they had one vital characteristic in common. That is, the significant business turnarounds achieved by these companies has been because of their holistic approach to organisational change: strategic choice, work organisation, company culture and organisational realignment have been conceived of and operationalised as complementary elements of competitive strategy.

The prime mover of contemporary organisational innovation has been the changed conditions of international competition, specifically the decline and fragmentation of previously stable mass markets: 'the new industrial competition'. Confronted with the entrance of significant new competitors, the secular decline and progressive decomposition of mass demand, innovative manufacturers are experimenting with methods of increasing productive flexibility, reducing the total cost of producing an extended and shifting product range for particular market niches rather than minimising the average output cost of a narrow range of standardised commodities (Sabel 1982). This is not to say that mass markets have entirely disintegrated or that economies of scale are now irrelevant to competitive performance. Rather, the balance between workforce rationalisation, the intensification of inherited work practices and the pursuit of new flexible patterns of work organisation is dependent upon the scale, scope and speed of the decline and decomposition of demand for an enterprise's core standardised products. The precise nature of this balance hinges upon a series of strategic choices linking novel and established marketing and production priorities within an overall change agenda. Thus, while flexibility is certainly a central concern of our case study firms it would be misleading to categorise work organisation in terms of two mutually incompatible strategies of 'Fordism' and 'Flexibility'. Developments in this area are taking place in the middle ground between these two extremes in firms which have not yet entirely renounced mass production as a guiding organisational principle but which are self-consciously promoting more flexible, responsive patterns of work organisation.

COMPETITIVE STRATEGY AND ORGANISATIONAL INNOVATION

A constant theme of this study has been the importance of work organisation in change agendas geared towards securing competitive advantage in uncertain market environments. The volatile market conditions of the 1980s have posed an enormous organisational challenge for each of our four case study firms. Ford's post-1980 experience stands in marked contrast to the 'rich complacency' of the 1970s: the company's entire product range was directly challenged by continental and Japanese competition. Ford's post-1980 marketing response has been twofold. First, heavy discounting to maintain domestic market share, a policy which inevitably depressed profit levels. Second, Ford initiated a radical redefinition of their central marketing strategy from mass production of standardised vehicles to a conception of the market as a complex amalgam of distinct segments demanding specific products. The combination of high volume production and niche marketing based on product differentiation through model derivatives has established the parameters of the change process in Ford since 1980 (Willman 1986, p. 211). Between 1960 and 1980 Pilkington dominated its core markets, glass and insulation, a dominance sustained by the company's technological superiority in product and processes. Rapid market growth and sector under-capacity encouraged Pilkington to expand and attracted new entrants to the marketplace without adversely effecting profits. However, Pilkington's core businesses were plunged into crisis in 1980-82 by the combined impact of the secular decline of the domestic motor industry and a sharp downturn in the insulation market, exacerbated by an abrupt change in government policy. Pilkington's marketing response has been the rapid renewal of its technological lead in its basic products and diversification through speciality, high value-added products. Shell shared the oil industry's traumatic experiences during the last decade and a half. Its marketing response has been to gradually alter the balance of its businesses, away from price sensitive, undifferentiated products towards higher value-added speciality oil derivatives and chemicals. In the capital intensive processing area, which remains Shell's mainstream activity, the long lead times for new plant have made rationalisation and paring labour costs vital competitive factors in the short and medium-term. The pattern of prolonged market leadership followed by a rapid decline in demand and profit growth was repeated in Rank Xerox which, similar to Ford and Pilkington, slid towards crisis after 1975. Struggling to retain market share in the face of significant, and growing, Far Eastern competition Rank Xerox responded with a proactive, niche marketing policy centred on meeting customer specifications for integrated office systems rather than maximising sales of standard products. Of our case study companies Rank Xerox's market situation was the most parlous and was met by the most ambitious change strategy.

Despite the broad similarities of the changed market conditions which have impelled organisational change Ford, Pilkington, Rank Xerox and Shell each pursued distinctive change strategies. In contrast to Pilkington, vital conceptual ingredients of the other two firms' change initiatives were derived from organisational links with multi-national corporations while Shell drew important lessons from its notable tradition of organisation development. As a result, the four firms comprise something of a spectrum, ranging from the experiential, deductive approach of Pilkington to the programmatic, inductive rationales which characterised both the Anglo-American initiative of Ford, with elements drawn 'After Japan', and, especially, the Anglo-Japanese strategy of Rank Xerox. Shell occupies the mid-point of this spectrum in that while the precepts of organisation development informed particular elements of the change process the company 'philosophy' remained strictly subordinate to strategic imperatives. Our intention has been to demonstrate that work organisation has been a central strand of the contrasting change strategies pursued by these innovating organisations; namely, Employee Involvement/Participative Management within Ford, the accelerated evolutionary development of Pilkington, the total process perspective of Rank Xerox and Shell's strategic organisation development. The conception and management of change in these organisations confirms the inadequacy of the structure-strategy, pioneered by Chandler (1962), paradigm either as a heuristic for understanding the process of innovatory change or as a prescriptive tool for enterprises searching for durable competitive advantage in volatile markets.

In our introductory chapter we aligned ourselves with the 'new consensus' among organisational theorists who dispute the ideas of rational decision-making, planning and organising which formed the substance of classical management thought. However, so deeply embedded are the implicit assumptions of the classical tradition that they are evident even in the work of those who ostensibly reject the strategy-structure paradigm. Thus, Pettigrew (1985), for example, offers a simple four stage model of the change process:

1. The development of concern by a subset of people in the organisation that, possibly as a result of environmental change, the present pattern of organising is incompatible with its operating environment.
2. The acknowledgement and understanding of the problem the organisation now faces, including an analysis of the causes of current difficulties, and alternative ways of tackling those difficulties.
3. Planning and acting to create specific changes as a result of preceding diagnostic and objective-setting work.
4. Stabilising the changes made by detailed implementation plans which include how the organisation's reward, information and power systems reinforce the intended direction of change (Pettigrew 1985, p. 434).

To be sure, Pettigrew quickly adds that the plans of the original innovative group may lie dormant awaiting sufficient political legitimacy within the organisation to become activated or may even be rejected outright, despite their accuracy, because of political coalitions of threatened functionaries. Nevertheless, whatever political complications might be introduced, the model itself is predicated upon overly rationalist assumptions about the nature of decision-making and its suggestion of a linear, if decidedly uncertain, progression from awareness to eventual actualisation.

Such an approach assumes that a change strategy is necessarily geared to achieving a particular, determinate objective, whether that be defined in terms of, for instance, market share or technical change. Such an assumption may have been appropriate to the relative stability of the competitive environment which prevailed until the mid-seventies but requires modification given the emergence of what Abernathy and colleagues (1978, 1981, 1983) term 'the new industrial competition'. In this competitive context modifying particular structural, cultural or technological features cannot, by itself, guarantee long-term market success. For the firms under study the underlying purpose of organisational change was to radically alter the terms of the innovation-efficiency dilemma by instilling a reflective capability at all levels of the organisation not just within strategic management groups. It was for this reason that senior managements were compelled – gradually in the case of Pilkington and Ford, explicitly in Rank Xerox and Shell – to recognise that organisations are characterised by inertia, slothful and adaptive change, and the chronic attachment to buried assumptions and routine behaviour. The key change problem, therefore, becomes intervention in organisational processes.

Organisational change was market-led in two senses; first, intensified competition in near saturated mature markets placed a high premium on maximising labour and capital productivity. Second, deteriorating market performance was paralleled by the increased importance of niche markets for speciality products. It was the dual nature of the marketing challenge confronting our case study organisations which ensured work organisation in the widest sense was ascribed high priority on corporate agendas. Increasing efficiency by intensifying existing divisions of labour and rationalisation was inadequate because such policies failed to address the strategic need to enhance organisational responsiveness to the shifting demands of a wider range of market niches. In each case, internal corporate and sectoral benchmarking was vital in identifying the scale of competitive disadvantage in terms of both productivity and flexibility. While productivity comparisons have a long history in Ford the last six years have witnessed a transformation of their role from the purely propagandistic to a central role in the change process. Indeed, productivity and flexibility benchmarking now occupies centre-stage in the company's internal collective bargaining. As a result of the international licensing arrangements for the float glass process Pilkington were uniquely well-placed to survey sectoral best practice. This international benchmarking exercise defined changing work organisation as the key to restoring Pilkington's competitiveness in a marketplace in which the main players shared common process and product technologies. Abstract comparisons were given internal credibility and political force by the introduction of new working patterns in a greenfield plant which then served as the basis for diffusion throughout the company. Competitive benchmarking has played an even more central role in Rank Xerox's change strategy. Rank Xerox's liaison with Fuji-Xerox has given it a vital window onto Japanese best practice in manufacturing and marketing. However, unlike Pilkington's benchmarking exercise which was based on crude physical output measures, Rank Xerox's emulative benchmarking involved identifying competitive gaps in design, manufacture, marketing and, most importantly, routine business administration. This process ensured that within Rank Xerox innovative capacity would not be sacrificed to reap short-term efficiency gains. Indeed, innovation in product, process and marketing was identified as the key to Rank Xerox's future commercial success. In a sector dominated by long-term overcapacity Shell identified rationalisation as the necessary response to short-term cost pressures while comparisons with continental production methods suggested that increased flexibility of capital stock and work organisation was essential to longer-term competitiveness.

Despite its shortcomings Pettigrew's simple model (Pettigrew 1985, p.434) does capture two essential elements of organisational change: while the impetus for change must come from corporate management the momentum of change is determined by their ability to secure workforce commitment to the change strategy. All the firms studied employed some kind of 'cascade' approach in which successive layers of managers and workers became involved in and, hopefully, identified with the change process. For Rank Xerox, based on the Fuji-Xerox exemplar, and Shell, drawing on their organisation development heritage, a cascade approach was deliberately deployed from the beginning of the change process in order to personally identify managers with the change strategy. Conversely, this policy was only adopted by Ford and Pilkington as a result of the educative experience of line management distancing themselves from change initiatives perceived to be imposed from above. In addition, securing operational management's commitment was vital to the success of the change programmes of each company since a common theme was the rapid decentralisation of important aspects of commercial and industrial relations decision-making. Further, workforce commitment to change was mobilised through the dissemination of business imperatives, a message given added weight by the reality of rationalisation in all cases. It should be noted that the threat of redundancy can secure labour compliance but not the commitment required to fully realise the productive and innovative potential of flexible work organisation. Significantly, Pilkington, Ford and Shell regard domestic collective bargaining as a crucial arena for building employee commitment, not as disparate centres of possible resistance to change. Of our case study companies, Rank Xerox has gone furthest in its attempt to develop a common set of analytical techniques to break down barriers between managerial groups and between management and labour by diffusing a shared understanding of the costs and consequences of change and stasis. Conversely, Ford have made the slowest progress in redefining its psychological contract with individual workers, a fact attributable to the deadening legacy of chronic low-trust labour relations and the fact that current prosperity is dependent upon maximising efficiency through maintaining tight labour discipline. In all cases management's prime concern has not simply been to push through a series of measures designed to increase productivity but to establish the structural, cultural and processual preconditions for ongoing change.

For each of our innovating organisations shifting managerial culture was regarded as essential to the success of the change process and coping with the new competitive environment. Two common features are particularly prominent. First, breaking down the narrow concerns of technical specialism protected by particular management groups and promoting increased business awareness, essential given that structural change decentralised important facets of commercial decision-making in all cases. Perhaps the most striking common indication of this new-found market awareness is in the companies' assimilation of consumers' variegated definitions of quality into production priorities irrepespective of the previously inviolable prerogatives of production engineers or accountants. In the process technology companies, Pilkington and Shell, the embedded organisational priority was on the subordination of financial and commercial considerations to those of operational expertise. This emphasis was particularly pronounced in Pilkington where for thirty years the company's success had rested on process and product innovation. In Shell, however, this technical bias was muted both by the powerful influence of organisational design and, in exploration and production, by the coordinative, quasi-entrepreneurial role of senior management of projects composed of company personnel and outside contractors. Second, as a corollary of the 'flattening' of internal hierarchies and a new 'customer-first' orientation, all managements experienced more cooperative, open relations between management groups which had previously been dominated by the political, protective stances of domain defence.

For companies pursuing marketing strategies of increased coverage of niche markets this 'customer-first' orientation was critical in giving different management groups a common focus beyond their immediate, vested interests. While this aspect of cultural change was apparent in all the companies it was most pronounced in Rank Xerox where the dissemination of the Leadership through Quality 'language' provided a shared framework for mutual problem-solving. Indeed, cultural change was an integral element of the Rank Xerox's total process change strategy. Pilkington, by contrast, had no pre-planned strategy for reordering managerial priorities and, like Ford and Shell, has adopted a more incremental, opportunistic orientation to fostering cultural change. Accordingly, managerial cooperation has developed slowly and fitfully within Ford where the long – and continued – dominance of short-term financial criteria for managerial decision-making has limited the immediate impact of the drive to foster participative management, although this drive still remains a core focus of its future change strategy. The reasons for the adoption of slow change strategies by Pilkington and Shell are somewhat different. In the former, fast change in company culture were discredited by the disappointments resulting from the failure of organisation development to live up to its early promise. In Pilkington, the principal reason for slow cultural change has been that so far the promoters of organisational innovation, although influential, remain relatively few in number. Essentially, Pilkington were faced with a choice between accelerating cultural change by spreading this innovative network thinly throughout the organisation and risk dissipating its force or progressing more slowly by devolving responsibilities and increasing its training commitment. Pilkington have chosen the latter 'slow but intense' process of achieving cultural change.

Our four case studies of organisational innovation share certain characteristics. Above all, changing work organisation, at both the levels of production process and managerial work, stemmed from the perception of rapid shifts in the contours of their core product markets; the decline and resegmentation of consumer demand and the entry of significant new competitors. To some degree, each company has reorientated its business strategy from product standardisation for stable, relatively homogeneous markets towards a more refined marketing strategy based on satisfying a range of finer market niches. This strategic reorientation has progressed furthest in Rank Xerox which has moved away from copiers as its core business to customer-specified integrated office systems. Strategic choice in Ford has involved an acceleration of the model replacement cycle and the production of high-specification derivatives of basic product ranges. Pilkington and Shell have initiated long-term changes in strategic direction towards higher value added speciality products. In this market context, competitive advantage hinges on achieving an optimal balance between the efficiency and responsiveness of work organisation, rather than simply maximising scale economies. In this sense, our case studies support Piore and Sabel's (1984) thesis that the 1980s constitute a transition period in business strategy, the end of Fordism and scientific management as the dominant paradigms of work organisation. For Piore and Sabel, the contemporary alternative to Fordism – 'flexible specialisation' – is implicit in the competitive strategies and work organisation of innovating companies. 'Flexible specialisation' refers to an integrated marketing, investment and production strategy which lies at the interface of product standardisation and customisation. Through the judicious mix of flexible computerised production technologies, upskilling and the sub-contracting of standardised component manufacture, innovating companies can better balance economies of scale and economies of scope in novel organisational configurations. In Ford, Pilkington, Rank Xerox and Shell the dominant marketing and production strategies of the 1970s were predicated on product market stability and the maximisation of scale economies through a highly integrated division of labour based on dedicated machinery, deskilling and direct managerial control. The key organisational task confronting innovating companies is the management of a portfolio of associated rather than standardised products in fluctuating batch sizes. In turn, this demands increased work organisation flexibility dependent upon the active cooperation of an upskilled, more versatile workforce and a move away from a rigidly bureaucratic and functional approach to management.

The extent of the companies' competitive disadvantage was revealed by internal and external benchmarking against sectoral best practice. Benchmarking represented a period of enforced introspection beginning at the strategic level and percolating through the organisation as the change process progressed. Pilkington's, Ford's and Shell's benchmarking exercises were confined to manufacturing costs and work organisation. In contrast, Rank Xerox instigated a more profound organisational benchmarking, isolating competitive gaps in all aspects of organisation not simply as a sporadic trigger exercise to prioritise change areas but as an on-going process. This contrast reflects the conceptual imperatives which underlay change in each company. In Rank Xerox change was conceptualised as a total process embracing strategic choice, technical innovation in product and process, work organisation and company culture. Self-consciously drawing on the experience of Fuji-Xerox, Rank Xerox accelerated the pervasive change process through the Leadership through Quality programme which propagated a common analytical language to maximise employee commitment to the process. Similarly, Ford's first change initiatives were based on the experience of the U.S. parent company. However, the failure of the 'After Japan' initiative in the context of the British industrial relations system forced Ford U.K. to retrench, then to introduce the long-term Employee Involvement strategy. In itself, this constituted a sharp break with Ford's traditional understanding of change in strictly structural terms, a break further reinforced by the development of Participative Management. Neither Pilkington nor Shell adopted a programmatic approach to change, preferring to accelerate evolutionary development: Pilkington's senior management are currently reviewing their post-1980 experiences with the intention of renewing the momentum of change within the company.

The process of change varied considerably between the four companies. In all four change was centrally directed but its momentum dependent upon the mobilisation of employee consent. Rank Xerox secured employee consent through the Leadership through Quality training.programme whose key function was to disseminate a common language to understand the necessity for and dynamics of the change process. In Pilkington trust building was facilitated by the joint union-management work reorganisation programme. Ford, by contrast, have been forced by the inertia of labour relations institutions to forego, at least temporarily, a programme-driven process of manufacturing consent. It remains to be seen how Employee Involvement develops. Overcoming the legacy of chronically low trust Industrial relations is necessarily a slow process but one which may be accelerated by the localisation of aspects of Industrial bargaining through the 1985 agreement. Underlying work reorganisation in each case has been the exposure of line management and shopfloor workers to market pressures either by organisational restructuring, as in Rank Xerox, or, as in Pilkington, Ford and Shell, through the demonstration effects of large-scale rationalisation.

In two of our cases a major impetus to change was new International standards of efficiency and product quality stemming from Japan. Japanese competitive advantage is generally attributed to the greater attention Japanese managers have paid to all aspects of work organisation (Beynon 1987). Dunning, in a study of the diffusion of Japaenese working practices in the U.K., has this to say about the relevance of the philosophy supporting this diffusion:

If this philosophy cannot ... be translated into the UK economy, this is not because of our ignorance of what needs to be done; but rather because of outdated traditions and values, Institutional rigidities or lack of motivation. It is this rather than anything else which is the British disease. (Dunning 1986, p.183).

Innovations in the companies we have studied have been aimed at curing this very disease.

To return to one of our starting points, the 'new consensus' in organisational analysis and its critique of structuralist approaches to organisational behaviour based on a rational economic model of decision-making. The 'new consensus' emphasises the importance of non-rational aspects of organisational behaviour, dimensions we have placed at the centre of our analysis of organisational Innovation. For Innovating organisations responding to the new challenges of Industrial dematurity, the key task is to mobilise those intangible social forces which promise a potential antidote to organisational Inertia. In their different ways, Ford, Pilkington, Rank Xerox and Shell have recognised the vital importance of harnessing employee commitment to company goals. Equally, corporate managers must be sensitive to the powerful Inertial forces Inherent in organisational cultures and ascribe as much Importance to Inculcating a culture of change throughout the organisation, not least in their Interactions with each other, as to their marketing or Investment strategies.

Appendix. Interview schedule

Our research is concerned with new forms of work organisation and the problems of managing these. We are particularly interested in changes in work organisation since 1980 — successes and failures, changes that have worked and innovations that haven't.

We would like to discuss any changes you have made in the areas of working practices, the relationship between management and labour, and the relationship between various managerial groups.

1. What changes have there been in your ways of organising work? Have there been any changes in the following areas?

A) <u>Rationalisation</u>
   size of organisation (lean-ness?)
   closures — redundancies
   rationalisation of space/ relocation

B) <u>Working practices</u>

   <u>skills</u>
   moves towards flexibility
   job redesign/ new working practices
   break down of previous demarcations (between and within trades/ between craftsmen and operators/ between craftsmen and white-collar staff)
   new emphasis on training

<u>new technology</u>
its effects on work organisation?
deskilling/ upskilling

<u>time</u>
more flexible approach to time - reorganisation of rotas, shifts
new balance of full and part time
new ways of contracting time

<u>sub-contracting</u>
more flexible use of sub-contracting

C) <u>More flexible management practices</u>

more flexible approach to management
alteration to the balance between centralisation and
decentralisation
new organisational structures
devolution of control
cultural change, e.g more participation, more consultation
stress on generalist management vs. functional specialism
Just in Time management principles

2. When were changes introduced? When did they become an important
part of the managerial agenda?
Was change incremental or was there a sudden, sharp turning point?

3. Why were the changes introduced? What problems were they
introduced to solve? To replace what outmoded practices?
(<u>Prompt</u>: competition/market-driven/efficiency/quality/flexibility

4. How much importance was attached to these initiatives in terms of
overall company strategy?

5. What happened in practice?
Where - generally or on which sites? (<u>Prompt</u> - greenfield sites)
Comparison of sites/ plants
Strategies for introduction.
Mechanisms, e.g., joint consultative procedures, quality circles,
job improvement committees?)
Formal agreements - with which unions?

6. Key sources of management information. Were did the new ideas come
from? (in-house - consultants?)
Was/ were the originator(s) of the ideas the moving force(s)
behind the implementation of the change(s)?

7. What resistance did the change(s) meet?
(<u>Prompt</u> - control issues/union resistance/management resistance

8. In what ways were work organisation changes integrated, if at all,
with business strategy? What mechanisms are there for making them
compatible? Key groups translating strategy into practice, e.g.,
personnel?

9. Are these new mechanisms?

10. How do you anticipate the changes proceeding? Do you anticipate
    new developments in the future? What? When? Why?

Bibliography

Abegglen, J.C. and Stalk, G., <u>Kaisha: the Japanese Corporation</u>, Harper and Row, London, 1986.

Abernathy, W.J., <u>The Productivity Dilemma. Roadblock to Innovation in the Automobile Industry</u>, John Hopkins, Baltimore, 1978.

Abernathy, W.J., Clark, K.B., and Kantrow, A.M. 'The new industrial competition' <u>Harvard Business Review</u>, October, 69–77, 1981.

Astley, W.G. and Van de Van, A.H., 'Central perspectives and debates in organization theory' <u>Administrative Science Quarterly</u>, 28, 245–273 1983.

Abernathy, W.J., Clark, K.B., and Kantrow, A.M., <u>Industrial Renaissance. Producing a competitive future for America</u>, Basic Books, New York, 1983.

Altshuler, A., Anderson, M., Jones, D., Roos, D. and Womack, J., <u>The Future of the Automobile</u>, George Allen and Unwin, London, 1984.

Barker, T.C., <u>The Glassmakers: Pilkington</u>, Weidenfeld Nicolson, London, 1977.

Bennis, W.G., 'Theory and method in applying behavioral science to planned organizational change' in Lawrence, J.R. (ed.), <u>Operational Research and the Social Sciences</u>, Tavistock, London, 1966.

Beynon, H., <u>Working for Ford</u>., Penguin, Harmondsworth, 2nd. ed., 1984

Beynon, H., 'Dealing with icebergs: organisation, production and motivation in the 1990s', Work, Employment & Society, 1, 247–259, 1987.

Blackler, F. and Brown, C., Whatever Happened to Shell's New Philosophy of Management?, Saxon House, Farnborough, 1980.

Blackler, F. and Shimmin, S., Applying Psychology to Organizations, Methuen, London, 1984.

British Institute of Management, Managing New Patterns of Work, British Institute of Management, London, 1985.

Burns, T. and Stalker, G.M., The Management of Innovation, Tavistock, London, 1961.

Chandler, A.D., Strategy and Structure: Chapters in the History of the American Industrial Enterprise, MIT Press, Cambridge, Mass., 1962.

Child, J., Organization. A guide to problems and practice, Harper and Row, London, 1977.

Child, J.C., Organization: practices and problems, Harper Row, London, 1984.

Clark, J., Technological Trends and Employment. 2. Basic Process Industries, Gower, Aldershot, 1985.

Clark, P. and Starkey, K., Organization Transitions and Innovation-Design. Pinter Publishers, London, 1987.

Confederation of British Industry, Managing Change: the Organization of Work, C.B.I., London, 1985.

Critchley, B. and Casey, D., 'Second thoughts on team building', Management Education and Development, 15, 163–175.

Crosby, P., Quality Is Free, McGraw Hill, New York, 1979.

Cross, M., Towards the Flexible Craftsman, Technical Change Centre, London, 1985.

Cusumano, M.A., The Japanese Automobile Industry. Technology and Management at Nissan and Toyota, The Council on East Asian Studies, Harvard University Press, Cambridge, Mass., 1985.

Cyert, R.L. and March, J.G., A Behavioral Theory of the Firm, Prentice Hall NJ, Englewood Cliffs, 1963.

Dunning, J.H., Japanese Participation In British Industry, Croom Helm, London, 1986.

Elger, T., 'Braverman, capital accumulation and deskilling' In Wood, S. (ed.), The Degradation of Work?, Hutchinson, London, 1982.

Flanders, A., *The Fawley Productivity Agreements*, Faber and Faber, London, 1964.

Foster, G., 'Rank Xerox's hard copy', *Management Today*, May, 60–65, 116, 120, 1987.

Galbraith, J.R., *Designing Complex Organizations*, Addison Wesley, Reading, Mass., 1973.

Giles, E. and Starkey, K. 'From Fordism to Japanization?', paper presented at Cardiff Business School 'Japanisation of British Industry' Conference, 1987.

Giordano, L., 'Beyond Taylorism: computerization and QWL programs in the production process', paper presented at the Aston/ UMIST Labour Process conference, Aston University, 1986.

Grikitis, K., 'Rooting out quality problems', *Electronics Manufacture & Test*, November, 1985.

Guest, R., 'Management imperatives in the year 2000', *California Management Review*, XXVIII, 4, 62–70, 1986.

Gyllenhammer, P., 'How Volvo adapts work to people', *Harvard Business Review*, July/August, 102–113, 1977.

Halberstam, D., *The Reckoning*, Bloomsbury, London, 1987.

Hartley, J., Kelly, J., and Nicholson, N., *Steel Strike. A case study in industrial relations*, Batsford, London, 1983.

Heydebrand, W.V., 'Technocratic corporatism. Toward a theory of occupational and organizational transformation' in Hall, R.H. and Quinn, E. (eds.), *Organizational Theory and Policy*, Sage, Beverley Hills, 1983.

Hickman, C.R. and Silva, M.A., *Creating Excellence. Merging corporate culture, strategy and change in the new age*, Allen and Unwin, London, 1984.

Hill, P., *Towards a New Philosophy of Management*, Gower Press, London, 1971.

Hill, S., *Competition and Control at Work*, Heinemann, London, 1981.

Hornby, D., 'Innovation into profit. "Can we teach ourselves to change?"' Royal Bank of Scotland Lecture, Aston University, 27 February 1986.

Institution of Production Engineers, *Organizational Change*, Institution of Production Engineers, London, 1980.

Jacobson, G. and Hillkirk, J., *Xerox. American Samurai*, Macmillan, New York, 1986.

Judkins, P., 'Towards new patterns of work', Rank Xerox, London, no date.

Judkins, P., West, D. and Drew, J., Networking in Organisations. The Rank Xerox Experiment, Gower, Aldershot, 1985.

Kanter, R.M., The Change Masters. Corporate entrepreneurs at work, Unwin Paperbacks, London, 1985.

Katz, H., Changing Gears: Changing labor relations in the US auto Industry, MIT Press, Cambridge, Mass., 1985.

Kilmann, R.H., Beyond the Quick Fix, Jossey–Bass, San Francisco, 1984.

Kolodny, H.F., 'Evolution to a matrix organization', Academy of Management Review, 4, 543–553.

Krijnen, H.G., 'The flexible firm', International Studies of Management and Organization, XIV, 64–90.

Lane, T. and Roberts, K., Strike at Pilkingtons, Fontana, London, 1971.

Lorenz, C., 'Full of Eastern promise — but handle with care', Financial Times, 27 January 1981, (a).

Lorenz, C., 'Why the quality revolution must start at the top', Financial Times, 4 February 1981, (b).

Lorenz, C., The Design Dimension. Product strategy and the challenge of global marketing, Blackwell, Oxford, 1986.

McLellan, S., The Coming Computer Industry Shakeout, Wiley, New York, 1984.

Marchington, M. and Parker, P., 'Japanization: a lack of chemical reaction?', paper presented at Cardiff Business School 'Japanisation of British Industry' Conference, 1987.

Marsden, D., Morris, T., Willman, P., Woods, S., The Car Industry. Labour Relations and Industrial Adjustment, Tavistock, London, 1985.

Mascarenhas, B., 'Flexibility: its relationship to environmental dynamism and complexity', International Studies of Management and Organization, XIV, 107–124, 1985.

Miles, R.H., Coffin Nails and Corporate Strategies, Prentice–Hall, Englewood Cliffs, NJ, 1982.

Miller, D. and Friesen, P.H., 'Momentum and revolution in organization adaptation', Academy of Management Review, 4, 591–614, 1980.

Miller, D. and Friesen, P.H., Organizations: a quantum view. Prentice Hall, Englewood Cliffs NJ, 1984.

Minkes, A.L. and Nuttall, C.S., *Business Behaviour and Management Structure*, Croom Helm, London, 1984.

Morgan, G., *Images of Organization*, Sage, Beverly Hills, 1986.

NEDO (National Economic Development Office), *Changing Working Patterns*, NEDO, London, 1986.

OECD (Organisation for Economic Cooperation and Development), *Petrochemical Industry. Energy Aspects of Structural Change*, OCDE, Paris, 1985.

Peters, T.J. and Waterman, R.H., *In Search of Excellence*, Harper and Row, New York, 1982.

Pettigrew, A.M., *The Awakening Giant. Contingency and change in ICI*, Blackwell, Oxford, 1985.

Pettigrew, A.M., 'Theoretical, methodological, and empirical issues in studying change: a response to Starkey', *Journal of Management Studies*, 24, 420-426, 1987.

Pettigrew, T.J., 'Process quality control: the new approach to the management of quality in Ford', *Quality Assurance*, 11, 3, 81-88, 1985.

Piore, M.J. and Sabel, C.F., *The Second Industrial Divide: Possibilities for Prosperity*, Basic Books, New York, 1984.

Porter, M.E., 'Competition in global industries: a conceptual framework' in Porter, M. (ed.), *Competition in Global Industries*, Harvard Business School, Boston, Mass., 1986.

Prahalad, G.K. and Doz, Y.L., 'Managing Managers: The work of top management', in J.G. Hunt et al (eds.), *Leaders and Managers: International Perspectives on Managerial Behaviour and Leadership*, Pergamon Press, Elmsford, New York, 1984.

Rank Xerox, 'Rank Xerox in Europe. A snapshot of 1985', Rank Xerox, London, 1985.

Roots, P., 'Collective bargaining: opportunities for a new approach', Warwick Papers in Industrial Relations, No. 5, 1986.

Ryan, P., *The Marketing of High Technology*, Institute of Electrical Engineers, London, 1984.

Sabel, C., *Work and Politics*, Cambridge University Press, Cambridge, 1982.

Strauss, A., and others, 'The hospital and its negotiated order' in Freidson, E. (ed.), *The Hospital in Modern Society*, Macmillan, New York, 1963.

Szilagyi, A.D., Jr., and Schweiger, D.M., 'Matching manager to strategies: a review and suggested framework', <u>Academy of Management Review</u>, 9, 626-637, 1984.

Tichy, N.M., 'Organizational cycles and change management in health care organizations' in Margulies, N. and Adams, J.D. (eds.), <u>Organizational Development in Health Care Organizations</u>, Addison-Wesley, Reading, Mass., 1982.

Tolliday, S. and Zeitlin, J., 'Between Fordism and Flexibility' in Tolliday, S. and Zeitlin, J. (eds.), <u>The Automobile Industry and its Workers</u>, Polity Press, Cambridge.

Tse, K.K., <u>Marks & Spencer</u>, Pergamon, Oxford, 1985.

Walton, R.E., 'From control to commitment in the workplace', <u>Harvard Business Review</u>, 63, 2, 77-84, 1985.

Waterman, R.H. Jr., Peters, T.J., and Phillips, J.R., 'Structure is not organization' in Herbert, T.T. and Lorenzi, P. (eds.), <u>Experiential Organization Behavior</u>, Macmillan, New York, 1981.

Weick, K., <u>The Social Psychology of Organizing</u>, Addison-Wesley, Reading, Mass., 2nd. ed., 1979.

Whipp, R. and Clark, P., <u>Innovation and the Auto Industry, Product, process and work organization</u>, Frances Pinter, London, 1986.

Williams, K., Williams, J. and Haslam, C., <u>The Breakdown of Austin Rover. A case study in the failure of business strategy and industrial policy</u>, Berg, Leamington Spa, 1987.

Willman, P., <u>Technological Change, Collective Bargaining and Industrial Efficiency</u>, Clarendon Press, Oxford, 1986.

Xerox Corporation, 'Leadership through Quality', Xerox Corporation, 1986.

Index